History & Geogra
Teacher's Guide Part 2

CONTENTS

Revision Editor: Alan Christopherson, M.S.

Alpha Omega Publications®

804 N. 2nd Ave. E., Rock Rapids, IA 51246-1759

HISTORY & GEOGRAPHY

Curriculum Overview
Grades 1–12

	Grade 1	Grade 2	Grade 3
LIFEPAC 1	**I AM A SPECIAL PERSON** • God made me • You are God's child • All about you • Using proper manners	**FAMILIES AND NEIGHBORS** • We need a family • We help our family • Our neighborhood • Helping our neighbors	**FISHING IN MAINE** • At look at Deer Island • A lobster boat • Planting lobster traps • Catching lobsters
LIFEPAC 2	**COMMUNICATING WITH SOUND** • Sounds people make • Sounds that communicate • Communicating without sound • Communicating with God	**COMMUNITY HELPERS** • What is a community • Community helpers • Your church community • Helping your community	**FARMING IN KANSAS** • The six parts of Kansas • Getting to know Kansas • Exploring Kansas • Harvest in Kansas
LIFEPAC 3	**I HAVE FEELINGS** • I feel sad • I feel afraid • I feel happy • I have other feelings	**NEIGHBORHOOD STORES** • Pioneer goods and services • Modern goods and services • Some business rules • God's business rules	**FRUIT-GROWING IN WASHINGTON** • Geography of Washington • Cities in Washington • Apple blossom time • Apple harvest time
LIFEPAC 4	**I LIVE IN A FAMILY** • My mother and father • My brothers and sisters • My grandparents • What my family does	**FARMS AND CITIES** • Farming long ago • Farming today • Growing cities • Changing cities	**FORESTS IN OREGON** • A land of forests • Trees of the forests • Lumbering in Oregon • Keeping Oregon's forests
LIFEPAC 5	**YOU AND GOD'S FAMILY** • Getting ready in the morning • Walking to school • The school family • The church family	**NEIGHBORS AROUND THE WORLD** • Things all families need • How communities share • How communities change • Customs of the world	**CALIFORNIA: A GOLDEN LAND** • Early California • The ranch community • A trip around the state • Work on a truck farm
LIFEPAC 6	**PLACES PEOPLE LIVE** • Life on the farm • Life in the city • Life by the sea	**A JAPANESE FAMILY** • Places people live in Japan • School in Japan • Work in Japan • Play in Japan	**CATTLE IN TEXAS** • Learning about Texas • Early ranches in Texas • Life on a ranch • A cattle round-up
LIFEPAC 7	**COMMUNITY HELPERS** • Firemen and policemen • Doctors • City workers • Teachers and ministers	**HOW WE TRAVEL** • Travel in Bible times • Travel in the past • Travel today • Changes in today's world	**COAL MINING IN PENNSYLVANIA** • The formation of coal • Products from coal • Methods of mining coal • The state of Pennsylvania
LIFEPAC 8	**I LOVE MY COUNTRY** • America discovered • The Pilgrims • The United States begin • Respect for your country	**MESSAGES FROM FAR AND NEAR** • Communication in Bible times • Communication today • Reasons for communication • Communication without sound	**MANUFACTURING IN MICHIGAN** • Facts about Michigan • Interesting people of Michigan • Places in Michigan • The treasures in Michigan
LIFEPAC 9	**I LIVE IN THE WORLD** • The globe • Countries • Friends in Mexico • Friends in Japan	**CARING FOR OUR NEIGHBORHOODS** • God's plan for nature • Sin changed nature • Problems in our neighborhoods • Helping our neighborhoods	**SPACE TRAVEL IN FLORIDA** • A place to launch spacecraft • Worker at the Space Center • The first flights • The trip to the moon
LIFEPAC 10	**THE WORLD AND YOU** • You are special • Your family • Your school and church • Your world	**PEOPLE DEPEND ON EACH OTHER** • Depending on our families • Depending on our neighbors • Depending on our communities • Communicating with God	**REVIEW OF NINE STATES** • California and Kansas • Washington and Maine • Oregon and Pennsylvania • Texas, Florida, and Michigan

Grade 4	Grade 5	Grade 6	
OUR EARTH • The surface of the earth • Early explorations of the earth • Exploring from space • Exploring the oceans	**A NEW WORLD** • Exploration of America • The first colonies • Conflict with Britain • Birth of the United States	**WORLD GEOGRAPHY** • Latitude and longitude • Western and eastern hemispheres • The southern hemisphere • Political and cultural regions	LIFEPAC 1
SEAPORT CITIES • Sydney • Hong Kong • Istanbul • London	**A NEW NATION** • War for Independence • Life in America • A new form of government • The Nation's early years	**THE CRADLE OF CIVILIZATION** • Mesopotamia • The land of Israel • The Nation of Israel • Egypt	LIFEPAC 2
DESERT LANDS • What is a desert? • Where are the deserts? • How do people live in the desert?	**A TIME OF TESTING** • Louisiana Purchase • War of 1812 • Sectionalism • Improvements in trade and travel	**GREECE AND ROME** • Geography of the region • Beginning civilizations • Contributions to other civilizations • The influence of Christianity	LIFEPAC 3
GRASSLANDS • Grasslands of the world • Ukraine • Kenya • Argentina	**A GROWING NATION** • Andrew Jackson's influence • Texas & Oregon • Mexican War • The Nation divides	**THE MIDDLE AGES** • The feudal system • Books and schools • The Crusades • Trade and architecture	LIFEPAC 4
TROPICAL RAIN FORESTS • Facts about rain forests • Rain forests of the world • The Amazon rain forest • The Congo rain forest	**A DIVIDED NATION** • Civil War • Reconstruction • Gilded Age • The need for reform	**SIX SOUTH AMERICAN COUNTRIES** • Brazil • Colombia • Venezuela • Three Guianas	LIFEPAC 5
THE POLAR REGIONS • The polar regions: coldest places in the world • The Antarctic polar region • Living in the grasslands	**A CHANGING NATION** • Progressive reforms • Spanish-American War • World War I • Roaring Twenties	**OTHER AMERICAN COUNTRIES** • Ecuador and Peru • Bolivia and Uruguay • Paraguay and Argentina • Chile	LIFEPAC 6
MOUNTAIN COUNTRIES • Peru – the Andes • Nepal – the Himalayas • Switzerland – the Alps	**DEPRESSION AND WAR** • The Great Depression • War begins in Europe • War in Europe • War in the Pacific	**AFRICA** • Geography and cultures • Countries of northern Africa • Countries of central Africa • Countries of southern Africa	LIFEPAC 7
ISLAND COUNTRIES • Islands of the earth • Cuba • Iceland • Japan	**COLD WAR** • Korean War and other crises • Vietnam War • Civil Rights Movement • Upheaval in America	**MODERN WESTERN EUROPE** • The Renaissance • The Industrial Revolution • World War I • World War II	LIFEPAC 8
NORTH AMERICA • Geography • Lands, lakes and rivers • Northern countries • Southern countries	**THE END OF THE MILLENNIUM** • Watergate and Détente • The fall of Communism • Persian Gulf War • Issues of the new millennium	**MODERN EASTERN EUROPE** • Early government • Early churches • Early countries • Modern countries	LIFEPAC 9
OUR WORLD IN REVIEW • Europe and the explorers • Asia and Africa • Southern continents • North America, North Pole	**THE UNITED STATES OF AMERICA** • Beginning America until 1830 • Stronger America 1830-1930 • 1930 to the end of the Millennium • The new Millennium	**THE DEVELOPMENT OF OUR WORLD** • Cradle of civilization • The Middle Ages • Modern Europe • South America and Africa	LIFEPAC 10

History & Geography LIFEPAC Overview

	Grade 7	Grade 8	Grade 9
LIFEPAC 1	**WHAT IS HISTORY** • Definition and significance of history • Historians and the historical method • Views of history	**EUROPE COMES TO AMERICA** • Voyages of Columbus • Spanish exploration • Other exploration • The first colonies	**UNITED STATES HERITAGE** • American colonies • Acquisitions and annexations • Backgrounds to freedom • Backgrounds to society
LIFEPAC 2	**WHAT IS GEOGRAPHY** • Classes of geography • Geography and relief of the earth • Maps and the study of our world • Time zones	**BRITISH AMERICA** • English colonies • Government • Lifestyle • Wars with France	**OUR NATIONAL GOVERNMENT** • Ideals of national government • National government developed • Legislative and Executive branches • Judicial branch
LIFEPAC 3	**U.S. HISTORY AND GEOGRAPHY** • Geography of the U.S. • Early history of the U.S. • Physical regions of the U.S. • Cultural regions of the U.S.	**THE AMERICAN REVOLUTION** • British control • Rebellion of the Colonies • War for independence • Constitution	**STATE AND LOCAL GOVERNMENT** • Powers of state government • County government • Township government • City government
LIFEPAC 4	**ANTHROPOLOGY** • Understanding anthropology • The unity of man • The diversity of man • The culture of man	**A FIRM FOUNDATION** • Washington's presidency • Adams administration • Jeffersonian Democracy • War of 1812	**PLANNING A CAREER** • Definition of a career • God's will concerning a career • Selecting a career • Preparation for a career
LIFEPAC 5	**SOCIOLOGY** • Sociology defined • Historical development • Importance to Christians • Method of sociology	**A GROWING NATION** • Jacksonian Era • Northern border • Southern border • Industrial Revolution	**CITIZENSHIP** • Citizenship defined • Gaining citizenship • Rights of citizenship • Responsibilities of citizenship
LIFEPAC 6	**U.S. ANTHROPOLOGY** • Cultural background of the U.S. • Native American cultures • Cultures from distant lands • Cultural and social interaction	**THE CIVIL WAR** • Division & Secession • Civil War • Death of Lincoln • Reconstruction	**THE EARTH AND MAN** • Man inhabits the earth • Man's home on the earth • Man develops the earth • The future of the earth
LIFEPAC 7	**ECONOMICS** • Economics defined • Methods of the economist • Tools of the economist • An experiment in economy	**GILDED AGE TO PROGRESSIVE ERA** • Rise of industry • Wild West • America as a world power • Progressive era	**REGIONS OF THE WORLD** • A region defined • Geographic and climate regions • Cultural and political regions • Economic regions of Europe
LIFEPAC 8	**POLITICAL SCIENCE** • Definition of political science • Roots of Western thought • Modern political thinkers • Political theory	**A WORLD IN CONFLICT** • World War I • Great Depression • New Deal • World War II	**MAN AND HIS ENVIRONMENT** • The physical environment • Drug abuse • The social environment • Man's responsibilities
LIFEPAC 9	**STATE ECONOMICS AND POLITICS** • Background of state government • State government • State finance • State politics	**COLD WAR AMERICA** • Origins of the Cold War • Vietnam • Truman to Nixon • Ending of the Cold War	**TOOLS OF THE GEOGRAPHER** • The globe • Types of maps • Reading maps • The earth in symbol form
LIFEPAC 10	**SOCIAL SCIENCES REVIEW** • History and geography • Anthropology • Sociology • Economics and politics	**RECENT AMERICA & REVIEW** • Europe to independence • Colonies to the Civil War • Civil War to World War II • World War II through Cold War	**MAN IN A CHANGING WORLD** • Development of the nation • Development of government • Development of the earth • Solving problems

Grade 10	Grade 11	Grade 12	
ANCIENT CIVILIZATION • Origin of civilization • Early Egypt • Assyria and Babylonia • Persian civilization	**FOUNDATIONS OF DEMOCRACY** • Democracy develops • Virginia • New England colonies • Middle and southern colonies	**INTERNATIONAL GOVERNMENTS** • Why have governments • Types of governments • Governments in our world • Political thinkers	LIFEPAC 1
ANCIENT CIVILIZATIONS • India • China • Greek civilization • Roman Empire	**CONSTITUTIONAL GOVERNMENT** • Relations with England • The Revolutionary War • Articles of Confederation • Constitution of the U.S.	**UNITED STATES GOVERNMENT** • U.S. Constitution • Bill of Rights • Three branches of government • Legislative process	LIFEPAC 2
THE MEDIEVAL WORLD • Early Middle Ages • Middle Ages in transition • High Middle Ages	**NATIONAL EXPANSION** • A strong federal government • Revolution of 1800 • War of 1812 • Nationalism and sectionalism	**AMERICAN PARTY SYSTEM** • American party system • Development political parties • Functions of political parties • Voting	LIFEPAC 3
RENAISSANCE AND REFORMATION • Changes in government and art • Changes in literature and thought • Advances in science • Reform within the Church	**A NATION DIVIDED** • Issues of division • Division of land and people • Economics of slavery • Politics of slavery	**HISTORY OF GOVERNMENTS** • Primitive governments • Beginnings of Democracy • Feudalism, Theocracy & Democracy • Fascism & Nazism	LIFEPAC 4
GROWTH OF WORLD EMPIRES • England and France • Portugal and Spain • Austria and Germany • Italy and the Ottoman Empire	**A NATION UNITED AGAIN** • Regionalism • The division • The Civil War • Reconstruction	**THE CHRISTIAN & GOVERNMENT** • Discrimination & the Christian • Christian attitudes • "Opinion & Truth" in politics • Politics & Propaganda	LIFEPAC 5
THE AGE OF REVOLUTION • Factors leading to revolution • The English Revolution • The American Revolution • The French Revolution	**INVOLVEMENT AT HOME & ABROAD** • Surge of industry • The industrial lifestyle • Isolationism • Involvement in conflict	**FREE ENTERPRISE** • Economics • Competition • Money through history • International finance & currency	LIFEPAC 6
THE INDUSTRIAL REVOLUTION • Sparks of preparation • Industrial revolution in England • Industrial revolution in America • Social changes of the revolution	**THE SEARCH FOR PEACE** • The War and its aftermath • The Golden Twenties • The Great Depression • The New Deal	**BUSINESS AND YOU** • Running a business • Government & business • Banks & Mergers • Deregulation & Bankruptcy	LIFEPAC 7
TWO WORLD WARS • Mounting tension • World War I • Peace and power quests • World War II	**A NATION AT WAR** • Causes of the war • World War II • Korean Conflict • Vietnam Conflict	**THE STOCK MARKET** • How it started and works • Selecting stocks • Types of stocks • Tracking stocks	LIFEPAC 8
THE CONTEMPORARY WORLD • The Cold War • Korean War and Vietnam War • Collapse of the Soviet Union • Today's world	**CONTEMPORARY AMERICA** • America in the 1960s • America in the 1970s • America in the 1980s & 1990s • International Scene 1980-Present	**BUDGET AND FINANCE** • Cash, Credit & Checking • Buying a car • Grants, Loans & IRAs • Savings & E-cash	LIFEPAC 9
ANCIENT TIMES TO THE PRESENT • Ancient civilizations • Medieval times • The Renaissance • The modern world	**UNITED STATES HISTORY** • Basis of democracy • The 1800s • Industrialization • Current history	**GEOGRAPHY AND REVIEW** • Euro & International finance • U.S. Geography • The global traveler • Neighbors, Heroes & The Holy Land	LIFEPAC 10

MANAGEMENT

STRUCTURE OF THE LIFEPAC CURRICULUM

The LIFEPAC curriculum is conveniently structured to provide one teacher handbook containing teacher support material with answer keys and ten student worktexts for each subject at grade levels two through twelve. The worktext format of the LIFEPACs allows the student to read the textual information and complete workbook activities all in the same booklet. The easy to follow LIFEPAC numbering system lists the grade as the first number(s) and the last two digits as the number of the series. For example, the Language Arts LIFEPAC at the 6th grade level, 5th book in the series would be LAN0605.

Each LIFEPAC is divided into 3 to 5 sections and begins with an introduction or overview of the booklet as well as a series of specific learning objectives to give a purpose to the study of the LIFEPAC. The introduction and objectives are followed by a vocabulary section which may be found at the beginning of each section at the lower levels, at the beginning of the LIFEPAC in the middle grades, or in the glossary at the high school level. Vocabulary words are used to develop word recognition and should not be confused with the spelling words introduced later in the LIFEPAC. The student should learn all vocabulary words before working the LIFEPAC sections to improve comprehension, retention, and reading skills.

Each activity or written assignment has a number for easy identification, such as 1.1. The first number corresponds to the LIFEPAC section and the number to the right of the decimal is the number of the activity.

Teacher checkpoints, which are essential to maintain quality learning, are found at various locations throughout the LIFEPAC. The teacher should check 1) neatness of work and penmanship, 2) quality of understanding (tested with a short oral quiz), 3) thoroughness of answers (complete sentences and paragraphs, correct spelling, etc.), 4) completion of activities (no blank spaces), and 5) accuracy of answers as compared to the answer key (all answers correct).

The self test questions are also number coded for easy reference. For example, 2.015 means that this is the 15th question in the self test of Section II. The first number corresponds to the LIFEPAC section, the zero indicates that it is a self test question, and the number to the right of the zero the question number.

The LIFEPAC test is packaged at the centerfold of each LIFEPAC. It should be removed and put aside before giving the booklet to the student for study.

Answer and test keys have the same numbering system as the LIFEPACs and appear at the back of this handbook. The student may be given access to the answer keys (not the test keys) under teacher supervision so that he can score his own work.

A thorough study of the Curriculum Overview by the teacher before instruction begins is essential to the success of the student. The teacher should become familiar with expected skill mastery and understand how these grade level skills fit into the overall skill development of the curriculum. The teacher should also preview the objectives that appear at the beginning of each LIFEPAC for additional preparation and planning.

TEST SCORING and GRADING

Answer keys and test keys give examples of correct answers. They convey the idea, but the student may use many ways to express a correct answer. The teacher should check for the essence of the answer, not for the exact wording. Many questions are high level and require thinking and creativity on the part of the student. Each answer should be scored based on whether or not the main idea written by the student matches the model example. "Any Order" or "Either Order" in a key indicates that no particular order is necessary to be correct.

Most self tests and LIFEPAC tests at the lower elementary levels are scored at 1 point per answer; however, the upper levels may have a point system awarding 2 to 5 points for various answers or questions. Further, the total test points will vary; they may not always equal 100 points. They may be 78, 85, 100, 105, etc.

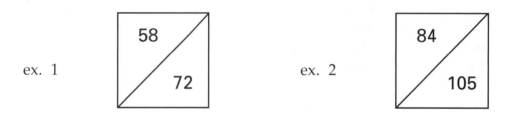

A score box similar to ex.1 above is located at the end of each self test and on the front of the LIFEPAC test. The bottom score, 72, represents the total number of points possible on the test. The upper score, 58, represents the number of points your student will need to receive an 80% or passing grade. If you wish to establish the exact percentage that your student has achieved, find the total points of his correct answers and divide it by the bottom number (in this case 72.) For example, if your student has a point total of 65, divide 65 by 72 for a grade of 90%. Referring to ex. 2, on a test with a total of 105 possible points, the student would have to receive a minimum of 84 correct points for an 80% or passing grade. If your student has received 93 points, simply divide the 93 by 105 for a percentage grade of 89%. Students who receive a score below 80% should review the LIFEPAC and retest using the appropriate Alternate Test found in the Teacher's Guide.

The following is a guideline to assign letter grades for completed LIFEPACs based on a maximum total score of 100 points.

LIFEPAC Test = 60% of the Total Score (or percent grade)
Self Test   = 25% of the Total Score (average percent of self tests)
Reports   = 10% or 10* points per LIFEPAC
Oral Work   = 5% or 5* points per LIFEPAC
*Determined by the teacher's subjective evaluation of the student's daily work.

Example:

LIFEPAC Test Score	=	92%	92	x	.60	=	55 points
Self Test Average	=	90%	90	x	.25	=	23 points
Reports						=	8 points
Oral Work						=	4 points

TOTAL POINTS   =   90 points

Grade Scale based on point system:

100	–	94	=	A
93	–	86	=	B
85	–	77	=	C
76	–	70	=	D
Below		70	=	F

TEACHER HINTS and STUDYING TECHNIQUES

LIFEPAC Activities are written to check the level of understanding of the preceding text. The student may look back to the text as necessary to complete these activities; however, a student should never attempt to do the activities without reading (studying) the text first. Self tests and LIFEPAC tests are never open book tests.

Language arts activities (skill integration) often appear within other subject curriculum. The purpose is to give the student an opportunity to test his skill mastery outside of the context in which it was presented.

Writing complete answers (paragraphs) to some questions is an integral part of the LIFEPAC Curriculum in all subjects. This builds communication and organization skills, increases understanding and retention of ideas, and helps enforce good penmanship. Complete sentences should be encouraged for this type of activity. Obviously, single words or phrases do not meet the intent of the activity, since multiple lines are given for the response.

Review is essential to student success. Time invested in review where review is suggested will be time saved in correcting errors later. Self tests, unlike the section activities, are closed book. This procedure helps to identify weaknesses before they become too great to overcome. Certain objectives from self tests are cumulative and test previous sections; therefore, good preparation for a self test must include all material studied up to that testing point.

The following procedure checklist has been found to be successful in developing good study habits in the LIFEPAC curriculum.

1. Read the introduction and Table of Contents.
2. Read the objectives.
3. Recite and study the entire vocabulary (glossary) list.
4. Study each section as follows:
    a. Read the introduction and study the section objectives.
    b. Read all the text for the entire section, but answer none of the activities.
    c. Return to the beginning of the section and memorize each vocabulary word and definition.
    d. Reread the section, complete the activities, check the answers with the answer key, correct all errors, and have the teacher check.
    e. Read the self test but do not answer the questions.
    f. Go to the beginning of the first section and reread the text and answers to the activities up to the self test you have not yet done.
    g. Answer the questions to the self test without looking back.
    h. Have the self test checked by the teacher.
    i. Correct the self test and have the teacher check the corrections.
    j. Repeat steps a–i for each section.

5. Use the SQ3R* method to prepare for the LIFEPAC test.
6. Take the LIFEPAC test as a closed book test.
7. LIFEPAC tests are administered and scored under direct teacher supervision. Students who receive scores below 80% should review the LIFEPAC using the SQ3R* study method and take the Alternate Test located in the Teacher Handbook. The final test grade may be the grade on the Alternate Test or an average of the grades from the original LIFEPAC test and the Alternate Test.

> *SQ3R: **S**can the whole LIFEPAC.
>   **Q**uestion yourself on the objectives.
>   **R**ead the whole LIFEPAC again.
>   **R**ecite through an oral examination.
>   **R**eview weak areas.

GOAL SETTING and SCHEDULES

Each school must develop its own schedule, because no single set of procedures will fit every situation. The following is an example of a daily schedule that includes the five LIFEPAC subjects as well as time slotted for special activities.

Possible Daily Schedule

8:15	–	8:25	Pledges, prayer, songs, devotions, etc.
8:25	–	9:10	Bible
9:10	–	9:55	Language Arts
9:55	–	10:15	Recess (juice break)
10:15	–	11:00	Mathematics
11:00	–	11:45	History & Geography
11:45	–	12:30	Lunch, recess, quiet time
12:30	–	1:15	Science
1:15	–		Drill, remedial work, enrichment*

*Enrichment: Computer time, physical education, field trips, fun reading, games and puzzles, family business, hobbies, resource persons, guests, crafts, creative work, electives, music appreciation, projects.

Basically, two factors need to be considered when assigning work to a student in the LIFEPAC curriculum.

The first is time. An average of 45 minutes should be devoted to each subject, each day. Remember, this is only an average. Because of extenuating circumstances a student may spend only 15 minutes on a subject one day and the next day spend 90 minutes on the same subject.

The second factor is the number of pages to be worked in each subject. A single LIFEPAC is designed to take 3 to 4 weeks to complete. Allowing about 3-4 days for LIFEPAC introduction, review, and tests, the student has approximately 15 days to complete the LIFEPAC pages. Simply take the number of pages in the LIFEPAC, divide it by 15 and you will have the number of pages that must be completed on a daily basis to keep the student on schedule. For example, a LIFEPAC containing 45 pages will require 3 completed pages per day. Again, this is only an average. While working a 45 page LIFEPAC, the student may complete only 1 page the first day if the text has a lot of activities or reports, but go on to complete 5 pages the next day.

Long range planning requires some organization. Because the traditional school year originates in the early fall of one year and continues to late spring of the following year, a calendar should be devised that covers this period of time. Approximate beginning and completion dates can be noted on the calendar as well as special occasions such as holidays, vacations and birthdays. Since each LIFEPAC takes 3-4 weeks or eighteen days to complete, it should take about 180 school days to finish a set of ten LIFEPACs. Starting at the beginning school date, mark off eighteen school days on the calendar and that will become the targeted completion date for the first LIFEPAC. Continue marking the calendar until you have established dates for the remaining nine LIFEPACs making adjustments for previously noted holidays and vacations. If all five subjects are being used, the ten established target dates should be the same for the LIFEPACs in each subject.

FORMS

The sample weekly lesson plan and student grading sheet forms are included in this section as teacher support materials and may be duplicated at the convenience of the teacher.

The student grading sheet is provided for those who desire to follow the suggested guidelines for assignment of letter grades found on page 3 of this section. The student's self test scores should be posted as percentage grades. When the LIFEPAC is completed the teacher should average the self test grades, multiply the average by .25 and post the points in the box marked self test points. The LIFEPAC percentage grade should be multiplied by .60 and posted. Next, the teacher should award and post points for written reports and oral work. A report may be any type of written work assigned to the student whether it is a LIFEPAC or additional learning activity. Oral work includes the student's ability to respond orally to questions which may or may not be related to LIFEPAC activities or any type of oral report assigned by the teacher. The points may then be totaled and a final grade entered along with the date that the LIFEPAC was completed.

The Student Record Book which was specifically designed for use with the Alpha Omega curriculum provides space to record weekly progress for one student over a nine week period as well as a place to post self test and LIFEPAC scores. The Student Record Books are available through the current Alpha Omega catalog; however, unlike the enclosed forms these books are not for duplication and should be purchased in sets of four to cover a full academic year.

WEEKLY LESSON PLANNER

Week of:

Subject	Subject	Subject	Subject
Monday			

Subject	Subject	Subject	Subject
Tuesday			

Subject	Subject	Subject	Subject
Wednesday			

Subject	Subject	Subject	Subject
Thursday			

Subject	Subject	Subject	Subject
Friday			

WEEKLY LESSON PLANNER

Week of:

	Subject	Subject	Subject	Subject
Monday				
	Subject	Subject	Subject	Subject
Tuesday				
	Subject	Subject	Subject	Subject
Wednesday				
	Subject	Subject	Subject	Subject
Thursday				
	Subject	Subject	Subject	Subject
Friday				

Student Name _____ Year _____

Bible

LP #	Self Test Scores by Sections 1	2	3	4	5	Self Test Points	LIFEPAC Test	Oral Points	Report Points	Final Grade	Date
01											
02											
03											
04											
05											
06											
07											
08											
09											
10											

History & Geography

LP #	Self Test Scores by Sections 1	2	3	4	5	Self Test Points	LIFEPAC Test	Oral Points	Report Points	Final Grade	Date
01											
02											
03											
04											
05											
06											
07											
08											
09											
10											

Language Arts

LP #	Self Test Scores by Sections 1	2	3	4	5	Self Test Points	LIFEPAC Test	Oral Points	Report Points	Final Grade	Date
01											
02											
03											
04											
05											
06											
07											
08											
09											
10											

Student Name _____   Year _____

Mathematics

LP #	Self Test Scores by Sections 1	2	3	4	5	Self Test Points.	LIFEPAC Test	Oral Points	Report Points	Final Grade	Date
01											
02											
03											
04											
05											
06											
07											
08											
09											
10											

Science

LP #	Self Test Scores by Sections 1	2	3	4	5	Self Test Points	LIFEPAC Test	Oral Points	Report Points	Final Grade	Date
01											
02											
03											
04											
05											
06											
07											
08											
09											
10											

Spelling/Electives

LP #	Self Test Scores by Sections 1	2	3	4	5	Self Test Points	LIFEPAC Test	Oral Points	Report Points	Final Grade	Date
01											
02											
03											
04											
05											
06											
07											
08											
09											
10											

TEACHER

N O T E S

25

INSTRUCTIONS FOR FIRST GRADE HISTORY & GEOGRAPHY

The first grade handbooks of the LIFEPAC curriculum are designed to provide a step-by step procedure that will help the teacher prepare for and present each lesson effectively. In the early LIFEPACs the teacher should read the directions and any other sentences to the children. However, as the school year progresses, the student should be encouraged to begin reading and following his own instructional material in preparation for the independent study approach that begins at the second grade level.

This section of the *Teacher's Guide* includes the following teacher aids: 1) Cumulative Word List 2) Teacher Instruction Pages.

The Cumulative Word List is made up of words introduced at least once in one of the ten subject LIFEPACs. An asterisk (*) following a word indicates a direction-word that the children will need to know by sight to complete the work independently. Sight words are words that either are needed before their phonetic presentation or do not follow the standard phonetic rules. These words need to be learned through memorization and children should be drilled on them frequently. The drill may be done by use of a chart posted in a prominent place, by word card drills, word recognition or meaning games. Some words on the Cumulative Word List are not expected to be part of the student's reading vocabulary but part of his speaking vocabulary for better understanding of subject content.

The Teacher Instruction Pages list the Concept to be taught as well as Student Objectives and Goals for the Teacher. The Teaching Page contains directions for teaching that page. Worksheet pages contained in some lessons follow this section and may be duplicated for individual student use. The Activities section at the end of each lesson is optional and may be used to reinforce or expand the concepts taught.

Materials needed are usually items such as pencils and crayons which are readily available. Additional items that may be required are writing tablets or any lined paper, alphabet cards, color and number charts, and flashcards for vocabulary words.

Page 1: PLACES PEOPLE LIVE

CONCEPTS: Children live in many different types of homes.

TEACHER GOALS: To teach the children about three different living environments.

READING INTEGRATION: vocabulary development, following directions, main idea, comprehension

VOCABULARY: live, work, play, farm, city, sea

MATERIALS NEEDED: pencils, crayons, poster paper, a copy of "The City Mouse and the Country Mouse" from *Aesop's Fables*

TEACHING PAGE 1:

Put the vocabulary words on the board. Say them out loud as you write them. After you read the top of page 1, see how many children have relatives living on a farm, living in a city, or by the sea. Questions you might ask are:

1. How would you get to school?
2. What would you do for fun?
3. What kinds of chores do you think you might have?
4. What types of food would you eat?
5. What would your house look like?
6. What types of pets would you have?
7. What would the weather be like?

PLACES PEOPLE LIVE

People live on farms.

People live in cities.

People live by the sea.

You will learn about where people live, where people work, and where people play.

 **Objectives**

1. I will know about farm life.
2. I will know about city life.
3. I will know about life by the sea.

page 1 (one)

ACTIVITIES:

1. *Packing:* What would the children pack in a suitcase if they were going to visit someone in the city, on the farm, or by the sea?

2. *Travel Posters:* Have each child design a travel poster that would depict vacationing in the city, by the sea, or on the farm.

3. *Read:* "The City Mouse and the Country Mouse" from *Aesop's Fables.*

PART I: Life on the Farm

Page 2 and 3: Life on the Farm/Home

CONCEPTS: Living on a farm.

OBJECTIVE: I will know about farm life.

TEACHER GOAL: To teach the children what farm life is like on a farm.

READING INTEGRATION: comprehension, main idea, following written and verbal directions, recalling details

VOCABULARY: barn, tractor, field, plant

MATERIALS NEEDED: writing tablets, Worksheets 1 and 2, (optional: Worksheet 3), pencils, crayons, scissors, brass tabs, glue or paste, drawing or construction paper

TEACHING PAGES 2 and 3:

Put the vocabulary words on the board. Have the children listen as you read each word out loud. Discuss each word with the children.

Choose a volunteer to read the text on page 2. Discuss things that are seen in the picture.

Read the text on page 3, or call on volunteers to read.

Ask: What is the large area of land around Stanley's home called?
What is a field used for?
Where do animals stay?
Why do animals need a barn?

I. LIFE ON THE FARM

People live on farms.
Farms have houses, barns, and animals.

page 2 (two)

HOME

Stanley lives on a farm with his family. They live in a house. There is a barn next to the house and a tractor in the yard. There are large areas of land around Stanley's home. These areas of land are called fields. Fields are used to plant corn, beans, and oats.

Animals stay in the barn. The barn keeps the animals dry when it rains.

page 3 (three)

ACTIVITIES:

1. *Writing tablet Exercise:* Dictate the vocabulary words to the class. Have the class write the beginning sounds of the words in their writing tablets.

2. *Do Worksheet 1.*

Ask the children to color the barn and the three animals on the wheel. Tell them to draw a fourth farm animal in the empty quarter of the wheel.

Instruct the children to carefully cut out the circle. Help them to cut along the three sides of the barn door so that the top half of the door will fold open.

Help the children punch a hole through the center of the wheel and through the matching hole below the hayloft. Tell them to line up the two holes and insert the brass tab. Make sure the tab is not so tight that the disc cannot be turned easily.

The children can then turn the disc and open the barn door to see which animal is in the barn.

3. *Do Worksheet 2.*

Tell the children to cut out the four pictures at the bottom of the page and to paste them in the correct home. When they have finished, have them color all of the pictures on the page.

Check the worksheet together and discuss what they know about each home.

Name _____

Who is in the barn?

Cut the barn door on the dotted line.

Cut out the circle.

History & Geography 106
Worksheet 1
232

Teacher check _____
Initial   _Date_

Name _____

Farm Homes

Color. Cut out. Match.

History & Geography 106
Worksheet 2
231

Teacher check _____
Initial   _Date_

4. *(Optional): Do Worksheet 3.*

Have the children make a rooster using the shapes on the worksheet. The teacher should have color pictures of roosters on display to help the class.

Tell the children to cut out the pieces on the page and to paste them onto drawing paper to form a rooster.

When they have finished, have them color the rooster and draw a background for it.

Name _____

Make a rooster.
Use these shapes.
Cut them out.
Paste them on drawing paper.

History & Geography 106

Worksheet 3

229

Teacher check _____
Initial   Date

Page 4: Activity Page

MATERIALS NEEDED: crayons, pencils, writing tablets, Worksheet 4

TEACHING PAGE 4:

Choose a volunteer to read the directions. Before instructing the children to get their crayons, discuss maps and the compass rose.

Say: A map is a picture. It is like a picture from high in the sky. A map shows everything flat. Some kinds of maps are called floor plans (map your bedroom or your classroom). Other maps you can draw include the school grounds, the neighborhood, or visit a farm and make a map of it!

Make a compass on the board. Tell the class they can find a similar compass on page 4. Explain that this compass tells the direction things can be found. There are four directions: north, south, east, and west.

Draw a simplified example of the worksheet on the board, using pictures different from those on the worksheet. Then help the children discover what direction each picture is, using the house as your reference point.

Discuss the picture on page 4. Allow students to complete the page independently. They may color the picture of Stanley's farm after completing the statements. Check it together. If needed, allow more time for children to color the picture.

ACTIVITIES:

1. *Writing tablet exercise:* Have children practice writing north, south, east, and west.

2. *Do Worksheet 4.*

Instruct the children to connect the dots and unscramble the mystery word. Talk about the purpose of a scarecrow. Point out that the long word has two smaller words in it. Ask the class what they are. Discuss what each word means.

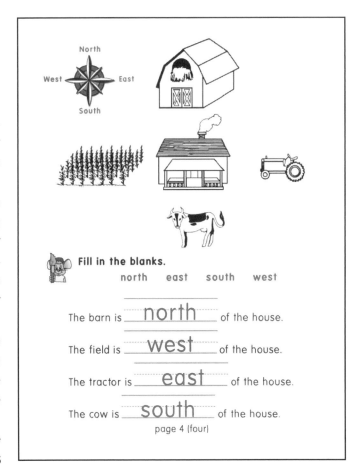

Fill in the blanks.

north   east   south   west

The barn is _____ north _____ of the house.

The field is _____ west _____ of the house.

The tractor is _____ east _____ of the house.

The cow is _____ south _____ of the house.

page 4 (four)

Name _____

What is in the garden? Connect the dots.

Unscramble this word.
CSARECRWO

scarecrow

History & Geography 106
Worksheet 4

Teacher check _____

230

33

Page 5: Work

CONCEPTS: Work is part of living on the farm.

OBJECTIVE: I will know about farm life.

TEACHER GOAL: To teach the children about the different types of work a young person will do on a farm.

READING INTEGRATION: main idea

VOCABULARY: chores, feeds, gathers, fence

MATERIALS NEEDED: writing tablets, ingredients for something made with milk and eggs, eggshells, coloring book, drawing paper, pencils, crayons, scissors, glue, Worksheet 5, (optional: Worksheet 6).

TEACHING PAGE 5:
Put the vocabulary words on the board. Have the children listen as each word is read out loud. Discuss the meaning of each word.

Ask several of the children to read the text out loud.
Ask: What can be made with the eggs Stanley gathers?
What kind of animal does Stanley have for a pet?

WORK

Stanley needs to help with the chores. Stanley feeds grain to the chickens. He also gathers the eggs.

Stanley goes into the barn. He asks if they need help milking the cows.

Stanley has a pet cow named Daisy. He gives Daisy a treat.

Then Stanley helps fix a broken fence.

page 5 (five)

ACTIVITIES:
1. *Sing:* "Old MacDonald Had a Farm" or "The Farmer in the Dell."
2. *Cook:* The class could make something good with milk and eggs (pancakes, scrambled eggs, cornbread, etc.)
3. *Make:* Use eggshells to make mosaics. Give each child a page from an easy coloring book to use for their eggshell mosaic.

4. *Do Worksheet 5.*

Tell the children to study the first picture strip carefully. Tell them they must complete the strip with the correct picture from the bottom of the page.

When they have completed the first strip, tell them to do the same with the second picture strip.

Check together. Have the children tell a story for each picture strip.

Give each child a sheet of drawing paper. Tell them that this time they have only the third picture (the bowl of fruit). Have them paste the picture on the right side of the paper. Tell them that they must draw two pictures that came *before* the bowl of fruit.

Since the story pictures will differ, give each child an opportunity to explain his picture strip. Have the children color all three stories.

More advanced students may select one story strip and write about it in their writing tablets.

5. *(Optional) Do Worksheet 6.*

This worksheet provides reinforcement with plurals. Before the children begin, encourage them to tell you what it is they are to do on the page. Point out "Words to Use" at the bottom of the page.

Check the worksheet together and give extra help to children who have difficulty.

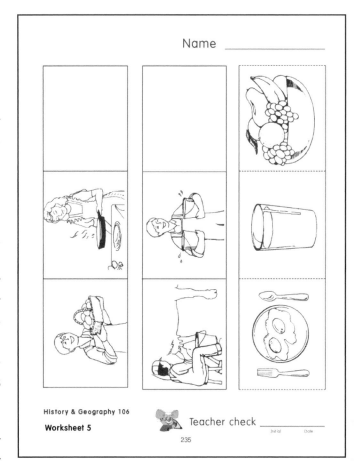

Page 6:

CONCEPTS: Work is part of living on the farm.

OBJECTIVE: I will know about farm life.

TEACHER GOAL: To teach the children about the different types of work a young person will do on a farm.

READING INTEGRATION: main idea, compare, contrast

VOCABULARY: grow, Review: tractor, field

MATERIALS NEEDED: Worksheets 7 and 8, (optional: Worksheet 9), styrofoam cups, bean seeds, potting soil, scissors, crayons, and glue.

TEACHING PAGE 6:

Write *grow* on the board and discuss. Review vocabulary words tractor and field. Write the words on the board and ask students to read the words. Then discuss each word.

Read the text aloud, or ask volunteers to read.

Ask: What are tractors used for?
What two things help seeds grow?

ACTIVITIES:

1. *Old and New:* On a sheet of drawing paper, have the children draw the old way of plowing fields (with horses or mules) on one side and the new way (tractor) on the reverse side. You could further this activity by doing a bulletin board of "old" and "new" ways on the fam. Remind the children that the "old" ways are still used successfully in some parts of our country and the world.

There are big fields around Stanley's farm. Stanley's parents plant corn and beans. The sun and rain help the seeds to grow. Then tractors are used to cut down the corn and beans.

page 6 (six)

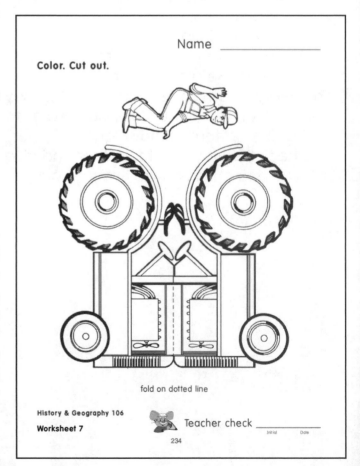

Name _____

Color. Cut out.

fold on dotted line

History & Geography 106
Worksheet 7

Teacher check _____
Initial   Date

234

36

2. Have the class grow a bean plant. This can be done as a class or individually. Use a styrofoam cup as the pot. Fill the cup with potting soil and plant the seed according to the directions on the package. Put the cup in a sunny place. Demonstrate how much water the bean seed needs. Allow children to water their plant(s).

3. *Do Worksheet 7.*

Have the children cut out and color the tractor. Then have them write one or two sentences about the tractor, or have them make a picture book showing things they can do with the tractor.

4. *Do Worksheet 8.*

Tell the children to look at the jumbled words at the top of the page.

Tell them that the words are unscrambled on the separate pieces at the bottom.

Instruct them to cut out the pieces at the bottom very carefully and to match them to the identical piece at the top. Before they paste the piece down, tell them to check that they have the correct unscrambled word.

When they have finished, have them read the words.

5. *(Optional) Do Worksheet 9.*

Put an example on the board to illustrate what is wanted on this "Before and After" activity. (Have the children supply the answers.) Check it together. Let the children explain their answers. If time allows, children may color the pictures.

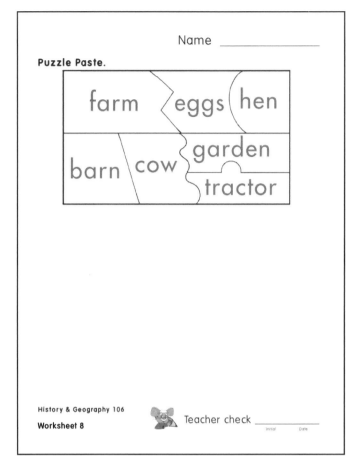

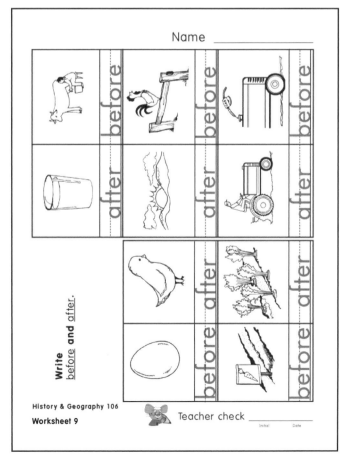

Page 7: Activity Page

MATERIALS NEEDED: pencils

TEACHING PAGE 7:

Discuss the matching pictures. Ask a volunteer to make the first match. Demonstrate how to match the items if necessary. Let the students complete this section independently. Go over the correct matches as a class.

Read the directions for the second section. Discuss the choices (*tractors, fields,* and *grow*). Read each sentence together and have the children give the answers.

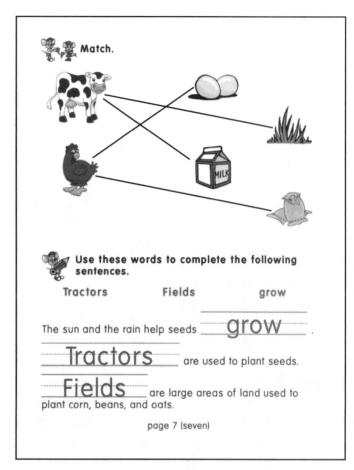

Match.

Use these words to complete the following sentences.

Tractors   Fields   grow

The sun and the rain help seeds ___grow___ .

___Tractors___ are used to plant seeds.

___Fields___ are large areas of land used to plant corn, beans, and oats.

page 7 (seven)

Page 8: Fun

CONCEPTS: Fun is part of living on the farm.

OBJECTIVE: I will know about farm life.

TEACHER GOAL: To teach the children the kinds of things young people do for fun on a farm.

READING INTEGRATION: following written directions, main idea, vocabulary development

VOCABULARY: yard

MATERIALS NEEDED: pencils, crayons, writing tablets

TEACHING PAGE 8:
Put the vocabulary word on the board. Have the children listen as you read the word out loud. Call on volunteers to describe a yard.

Have volunteers read the text on page eight out loud.

Read the directions in the middle of the page.

Ask volunteers to share their ideas with the class. Allow students time to complete their drawings. Ask if anyone wants to share their drawing with the class.

ACTIVITY:
Writing tablet: Write sentences together, sounding out each word and reinforcing spelling rules that have been learned so far. Have students write the sentences in their writing tablets:
Stanley and I would play _____ .
I would ride bikes with Stanley.

FUN

Stanley has fun on the farm. He has a big yard to play in.

He plays on his swing.

He plays ball with his family.

Draw a picture of what you would do if you could play with Stanley on the farm.

page 8 (eight)

Page 9: Fun

CONCEPTS: Fun is part of living on the farm.

OBJECTIVE: I will know about farm life.

TEACHER GOAL: To teach the children the kinds of things young people do for fun on a farm.

READING INTEGRATION: main idea, vocabulary development

VOCABULARY: fair, pen

MATERIALS NEEDED: writing tablets, construction paper, recipe and ingredients, clay

TEACHING PAGE 9:
Write the vocabulary words on the board. Read and discuss the words. Have children write the words in their writing tablets.
Ask for volunteers to read page 9. Discuss the fair.

> *Ask:* Has anyone been to a fair? What kinds of things did you see there? Possible answers: *animals, contests (pie eating, quilts, etc.), games (Bingo), rides.*

ACTIVITIES:
1. *4-H Club:* Look into the 4-H Club in your area. Have one of the people come out and talk to the children about the club.
2. *Fair Fun:* At the fair you see many types of contests going on. Here are a few mock situations your class may enjoy doing. Give out blue, red, and white ribbons for prizes. Let the class be your judges.

Stanley gets to go to the fair. He gets to bring Daisy for the animal show.

Stanley helps put Daisy in her pen. He makes sure she has water to drink and hay to eat. Then he goes on rides.

page 9 (nine)

a. *Quilt Contest:* Have the children construct mini-quilt designs using construction paper and odds and ends. Be sure to show the children pictures of quilts so they understand what they are before they begin.

b. *Recipe Contest:* One of two options:
(1) Children bring in samples of favorite recipes for the class to taste and judge.
(2) Divide the children into teams. Have each team make the same recipe. Allow children to judge.

c. *Clay Animal Contest:* Each child constructs some type of farm animal out of clay. The class judges them using ribbons as prizes.

Pages 10 and 11: Self Test 1

CONCEPTS: evaluation

OBJECTIVE: I will know about farm life.

TEACHER GOAL: To check each child's progress.

BIBLE REFERENCES: Psalm 23, stories of David tending sheep; Ruth; stories about Jesus that deal with farm images

READING INTEGRATION: following written and oral directions

VOCABULARY: Review all vocabulary words in Part One.

MATERIALS NEEDED: pencils, writing tablet, Worksheet 10, scissors, glue, and crayons.

TEACHING PAGES 10 AND 11:

1. Have the children turn to page 10 in their LIFEPACs. Read the directions for pages 10 and 11 together. Answer any questions about what to do. Identify all illustrations. Allow the children sufficient time to complete. Check as soon as possible after children are finished.

2. *Writing tablet Exercise:* Put scrambled vocabulary words on the board for the children to copy correctly in their writing tablets. Discuss the meaning of words as they are identified.

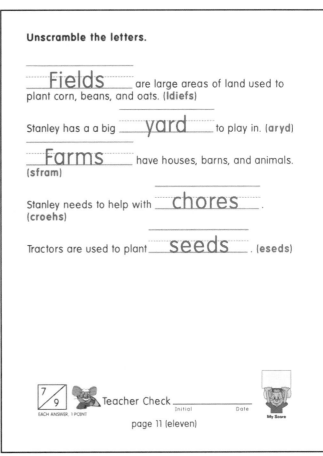

3. *Do Worksheet 10.*
Have the children color the pictures, cut them out, and paste or tape the bands to fit their fingers.

a. Have them create and act out stories about farm animals.

b. Have them sing and act out "Old MacDonald Had a Farm."

4. Write several vocabulary words on small pieces of paper and put them in a paper sack. Have each child in the class draw one word from the sack and write a sentence about it. The teacher may wish to have the children read their sentence out loud.

5. *Farm Faith:* (Stories, verses, and activities from the Bible.) Explain to the children that many stories in the Bible tell about farm life long ago.

a. Tell the story of how the farmer Boaz and Ruth met (from the Book of Ruth).

b. Tell the story of the farmer's son, David. Have the children draw a picture of David tending the sheep. Paste cotton on the drawings of the sheep.

c. Tell the story of Jesus being born in a stable. Help them to construct a diorama or draw a picture of the stable scene.

5. Discuss foods that would be made on a farm (homemade bread, jam, and ice cream; home canned vegetables, etc.) and share with students how they are prepared.

Name _____

Finger Puppets

PASTE PASTE
PASTE PASTE
PASTE PASTE
PASTE PASTE

History & Geography 106
Worksheet 10

Teacher check _____
Initial   Date

242

PART II: Life in the City

Pages 12 and 13: Life in the City/Home

CONCEPTS: Living in a city.

OBJECTIVE: I will know about city life.

TEACHER GOAL: To teach the children what life is like in the city.

READING INTEGRATION: main idea, compare and contrast

VOCABULARY: apartment, business

MATERIALS NEEDED: Worksheet 11, crayons or markers, scissors, glue.

TEACHING PAGES 12 AND 13:

Put the vocabulary words on the board. Have the children listen as you read each word out loud. Teach the children how to clap out the syllables with their hands. Then clap out the vocabulary words. Talk about where the words might be broken up. Discuss the meaning of each word.

Ask the children if they think living in the city is going to be like living on a farm. Read page 12 out loud.

> *Ask:* What does the city have that the farm also has? *(houses, fun things to do)*
>
> What are businesses?

Choose children from the class to read the text on page thirteen.

II. LIFE IN THE CITY

People live in cities.
Cities have houses, businesses, and fun things to do.

page 12 (twelve)

HOME

There are homes in the city. Some people live in houses. Other people live in apartment buildings.

Apartment buildings are large buildings. They have many homes in them. Many families can live in the same apartment building.

page 13 (thirteen)

ACTIVITY:

Do Worksheet 11.

After the children have cut and pasted the worksheet, ask them these questions:

"What floor is apartment six on?"

"What floor is apartment one on?"

"Do the apartment numbers get bigger or smaller as you go higher?"

"How many apartments are in this building?"

"Is the door with number ten on it an apartment?"

"How many floors are in this building?"

"How do you think the people get to the different floors?"

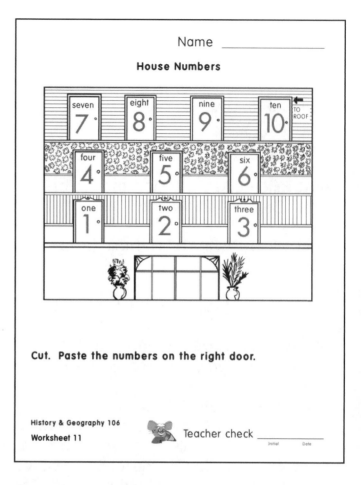

Name _____

House Numbers

Cut. **Paste the numbers on the right door.**

History & Geography 106
Worksheet 11

Teacher check _____
Initial   Date

Pages 14 and 15:

CONCEPTS: Living in a city.

OBJECTIVE: I will know about city life.

TEACHER GOAL: To teach the children what life is like in the city.

READING INTEGRATION: main idea, compare and contrast

VOCABULARY: family, friend, next door

MATERIALS NEEDED: pencils, old magazines, Worksheet 12, crayons, and glue.

TEACHING PAGES 14 AND 15:
Say each vocabulary word out loud. Have the students listen for the beginning sound. Write each word on the board and discuss.

Read page 14 out loud, or ask for volunteers to read.

Ask: How is living in the city like living on a farm?

How is living in the city different than living on a farm?

If children are having difficulty coming up with similarities and differences, ask more specific questions.

Ask: Can children have pets in the city? Would they have a cow?

What kind of pets do children have in the city?

Do you see tractors in the city?

What kind of vehicles do you see in the city?

Read the directions on page 15. Read the first statement and answer choices. Allow children time to circle the answer. Repeat this process for the next two statements. Go back to the first statement and ask a child to give the answer. Give feedback such as, *"You're right. Lisa lives in a house."* Repeat this process for the last two statements.

Lisa lives in a house in the city. She lives with her parents and her younger brother. This is Lisa's family.

page 14 (fourteen)

There are other houses all around Lisa's house. Lisa likes to sit on her front steps and talk with her friend. Her friend lives in the house next door.

 **Circle the correct answer.**

Lisa lives in _____ .
(a house)   an apartment building

Lisa lives with her _____ .
friend   (family)

Lisa's friend lives in the house _____ .
across town   (next door)

page 15 (fifteen)

ACTIVITY:

1. *Bulletin Board:* Make a bulletin board showing Lisa's street/city (houses, trees, street, stores, and a park). Have the children cut out appropriate pictures from magazines to paste in the store windows.

2. *Do Worksheet 12.*
 Have a discussion about the kinds of pets people can have in the city. Then have the children cut, paste, and color the worksheet.

Discuss the care of each kind of pet, the food they eat, and the type of home they need.

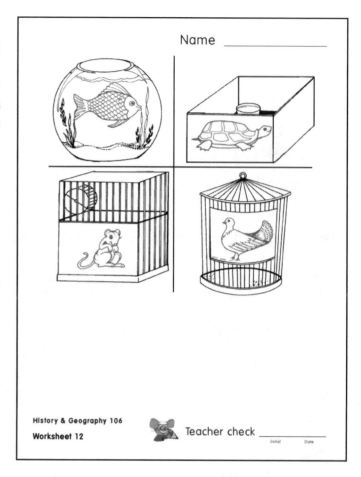

Name _____

History & Geography 106
Worksheet 12

Teacher check _____
Initial   Date

Pages 16 and 17: Work

CONCEPTS: Work is part of living in the city.

OBJECTIVE: I will know about city life.

TEACHER GOAL: To teach the children about types of work done in the city.

READING INTEGRATION: main idea, reasoning

VOCABULARY: office, clean

MATERIALS NEEDED: pencils, crayons, scissors, glue writing tablets, Worksheet 13, (optional: Worksheet 14),

TEACHING PAGES 16 AND 17:
Write the vocabulary words on the board. Pronounce each word aloud Have the children clap their hands to show how many syllables each of the vocabulary words has. Ask volunteers to explain the meaning of each word.

Ask for volunteers to read the text on page 16. Discuss the pictures.

Ask: What kinds of things do you see in an office? *(computers, telephones, papers, etc.)*
What kinds of things are sold in stores? *(groceries, clothes, books, toys, etc.)*

Ask a volunteer to read the top of page 17. Ask children to share things that they do to help around the house.

Read the directions in the middle of the page. Start a few sentences together on the board.

Lisa helps clean _____ .
Lisa washes _____ .

Have children write a sentence of their own using one of the models on the board. Allow time for children to draw and color a picture about their sentence.

WORK

There are many businesses in the city. Some businesses are in tall buildings. These buildings are full of offices. People work in offices.

People also work in stores. There are many stores in the city.

page 16 (sixteen)

Lisa works around the house. She needs to take out the trash and keep her room clean.

Can you think of one more thing Lisa could do around the house?

 Write a sentence.

Teacher check

 Draw a picture.

page 17 (seventeen)

ACTIVITIES:

1. *Writing tablet Exercise:* On the board print the words *in, out,* and *around.* Dictate these sentences to the class and have the children copy the missing word in their writing tablets using the words on the board.

People work _____ offices. *(in)*
Lisa works _____ the house. *(around)*
Lisa takes _____ the trash. *(out)*

2. *Basic Shapes:* Draw a large square, circle, triangle, and rectangle on the board. Write a set of four words in each shape. Read all of the words together. Ask a volunteer to come to the board and cross out the word that does not belong in the first shape. Discuss the reason why that word does not belong. Continue this process with the remaining shapes.

Shape 1: live, tractor, work, play
Shape 2: feeds, gathers, apartment, cleans
Shape 3: house, plant, apartment, building
Shape 4: front steps, fence, yard, grow

3. *Do Worksheet 13.* Have the children cut off the top part of the worksheet and paste it on a larger piece of paper. Then have them cut out vehicles that you would find in the city and paste them on the paper. Talk about what each vehicle does to help the city.

Ask where the remaining machines belong *(tractor—farm; sailboat—sea; wheelbarrow—farm).*

4. *(Optional) Do Worksheet 14.* This Worksheet provides practice on words that end with *sh.*

Have the children color the sweeper.
Have them cut out the strip.
Help them to cut the two slots in the sweeper.
Tell them to slide the word strip through the vacuum and read the words that they "sweep up."

Name _____

City Wheels

History & Geography 106
Worksheet 13

Teacher check _____
Initial   Date

247

Name _____

Sweep up the words.

trash

crash

dash

mash

wash

flash

sash

dish

fish

←— cut —→

History & Geography 106
Worksheet 14

Teacher check _____
Initial   Date

248

Page 18: Fun

CONCEPTS: Fun is part of living in the city.

OBJECTIVE: I will know about city life.

TEACHER GOAL: To teach the children what city children do to have fun.

READING INTEGRATION: main idea, following directions

VOCABULARY: museum, restaurant

MATERIALS NEEDED: Computer with internet access, pencils, construction paper, old magazines, scissors, glue, crayons, tablecloths, toy register, play money, Worksheets 15 and 16.

TEACHING PAGE 18:

Write the vocabulary words on the board. Have the children listen as you read each word out loud. Discuss the words. Ask students if they have been to museums and restaurants. Discuss different things that museums have (art, dinosaurs, old artifacts, etc.). Ask for volunteers to read page 18. Ask if children have been to the zoo or an amusement park. Allow time for sharing their experiences. Discuss other things that Lisa and her friends could do at the park.

ACTIVITIES:

1. Search the internet for popular museums. Show the children pictures of what these museums have on display.

2. Take a trip to a nearby museum or zoo.

3. Have students create menus including their favorite foods. Fold a piece of construction paper in half. Write the title of the restaurant on the front. Write the meals on the inside and drinks and desserts on the back. You may also

FUN

There are many fun things to do in the city. Cities have museums and restaurants. Lisa enjoys going to her favorite restaurant with her family.

Children in the city enjoy going to the zoo and amusement parks.

Lisa likes to go to the park with her friends. They swing and go down tall slides.

page 18 (eighteen)

have the children cut out pictures from magazines or draw pictures to illustrate menu choices rather than writing them.

4. Set up a restaurant in the classroom. Cover tables with tablecloths, and have a toy cash register with play money. Display menus.

a. Allow students to play in the restaurant in their spare time.

b. Use the restaurant as a math enrichment activity. Assign simple prices to meals, drinks, and desserts. Split the children into two groups: customers and waiters/waitresses. Have the customers order from a menu and the servers add up the total cost. Customers then pay for their meal. The servers need to make sure the money amount is correct. Switch player roles, allowing children to be both a customer and a server.

5. *Do Worksheet 15.* This worksheet has two game sets, one for home and one for school.

Have the children cut out the game cards and mount them on separate sheets of poster board.

Have them count out one set of playing cards and put them in an envelope. Then have them do the same with the second set of cards.

To play the game: Each child has a zoo card and a small deck of 12 cards. They each shuffle their own decks and lay them face down to draw from. If they draw a zoo animal, they put it in the zoo. If not, they discard the card in a discard pile. The first zoo keeper to get all six of his animals back in the zoo wins.

6. *Do Worksheet 16.* Write the words *above, below,* and *beside* on the board. Be sure the children understand each of these positional words.

Allow children time to cut out each of the cages.

Read the directions together, allowing children time to paste the cages into the correct slots.

Check their work together.

Let students color the pictures.

7. *Zoo Fun:* Do a bulletin board displaying each child's favorite zoo animal. Have them draw their favorite animal, or find a picture of the animal from an old magazine. Make the board look like a large cage.

Name _____

Play Zoo Keeper

Game card #1 | Game card #2

SET TWO

SET ONE

History & Geography 106
Worksheet 15

Teacher check _____
Initial   Date

251

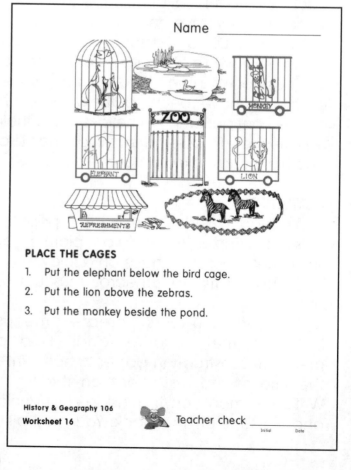

Name _____

PLACE THE CAGES

1. Put the elephant below the bird cage.

2. Put the lion above the zebras.

3. Put the monkey beside the pond.

History & Geography 106
Worksheet 16

Teacher check _____
Initial   Date

Page 19:

CONCEPTS: Fun is part of living in the city.

OBJECTIVE: I will know about city life.

TEACHER GOAL: To teach the children what city children do to have fun.

READING INTEGRATION: main idea

TEACHING PAGE 19:

Read the directions and discuss all the pictures. Allow children time to complete the activity. Check together.

ACTIVITIES:

1. *Fun at the park:*

a. Go to a nearby park and allow children to play.

b. Plan a picnic at the park.

2. *Writing tablet Exercise:* Have the children write two questions they would ask Lisa about living in the city.

Draw a circle around the things Lisa likes to do.

page 19 (nineteen)

Pages 20 and 21: Self Test 2

CONCEPTS: evaluation

OBJECTIVE: I will know about city life.

TEACHER GOAL: To check each child's progress.

BIBLE REFERENCES: Book of Joshua, Luke 2:42–52, Book of Revelation

VOCABULARY: Review all vocabulary.

MATERIALS NEEDED: pencils, Bible

TEACHING PAGES 20 AND 21:

Read all the directions and any words the children find difficult. Discuss each picture.

Let the children do the Self Test independently.

Check together. Review any concepts that were missed.

ACTIVITY:

1. *City Faith*: The Bible talks about or refers to life in the city. Here are a few to discuss with the class:

    a. Book of Joshua (city of Jericho)

    b. Luke 2:42–52 (Jesus' visit to the city of Jerusalem

    c. Book of Revelation (God's beautiful city of the future)

    d. Zoo animals in the Bible: lions in the Book of Daniel. Other animals in the Bible that can be found at a city zoo are camels, sheep, goats, and horses. Have the children put together a book called "Animals of the Bible." They may use pictures from old magazines or draw them.

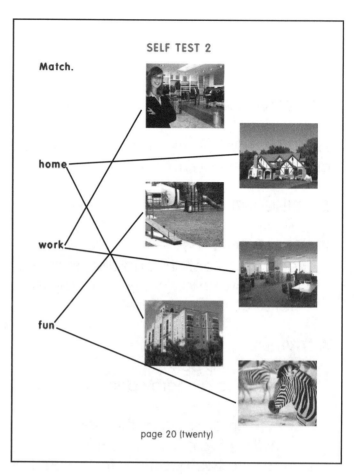

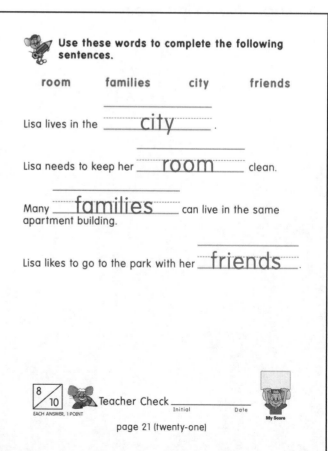

Part III: Life by the Sea

Page 22 and 23: Life by the Sea/Home

CONCEPTS: Living by the sea.

OBJECTIVE: I will know about life by the sea.

TEACHER GOAL: To teach the children what a home by the sea is like.

READING INTEGRATION: main idea

VOCABULARY: lighthouse, seagulls

MATERIALS NEEDED: crayons, scissors, Worksheet 17

TEACHING PAGES 22 AND 23:
Write the vocabulary words on the board. Have the children listen as you read each word out loud. Have pictures of lighthouses available for the children to see.

Choose children from the class to read the text on pages 22 and 23. Discuss the environment by the sea. Ask if anyone has been to the ocean. Ask what kinds of things someone might see at the sea/ocean.

ACTIVITY:
1. *Sea or See:* Discuss that even though *sea* and *see* sound the same, they are not spelled the same. Explain *sea* as a big body of water and *see* as what we do with our eyes. Put sentences on the board. Call on volunteers to come to the board and write in the correct word.

Josh lives by the _____ . *(sea)*
Josh can _____ a lighthouse. *(see)*
Josh can _____ boats. *(see)*
Seagulls live by the _____ . *(sea)*

III. LIFE BY THE SEA

People live by the sea.
The sea has lighthouses, boats, and beaches.

page 22 (twenty-two)

HOME

Josh lives by the sea. There are big rocks along the water.

White birds land in Josh's yard. These birds are called seagulls. Josh feeds bread to the seagulls.

Josh can see a lighthouse from his home.

page 23 (twenty-three)

---

2. *Do Worksheet 17.*

Instruct the children to cut out the light-house insert and assist them in cutting the slots in the lighthouse. Have the children color the lighthouse. Explain how light-houses function and discuss when the lighthouse is actually "lit." The lighthouse can be "lit" for night use by pulling on the insert so that the lit bulb is visible. During the daytime, the light can be turned off by pulling on the insert so that the darkened bulb is visible.

Name _____

Cut out

PULL ↕

cut

cut

History & Geography 106

Worksheet 17

254

Teacher check _____

Initial   Date

Page 24: Activity Page

READING INTEGRATION: following written directions

MATERIALS NEEDED: crayons

TEACHING PAGE 24:

Tell the students that they are about to color a picture, but that they have to follow the directions. Ask volunteers to read each line of the directions. After each line has been read, identify that object in the picture. Allow students time to color. Monitor student progress and ability to follow instructions.

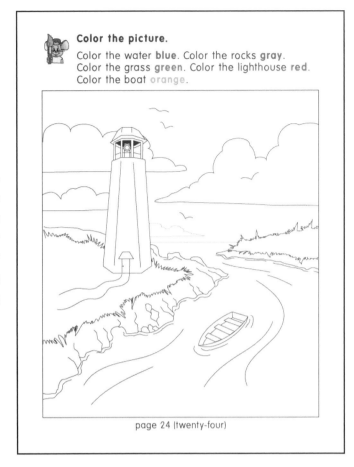

Color the picture.
Color the water **blue**. Color the rocks **gray**.
Color the grass **green**. Color the lighthouse **red**.
Color the boat orange.

page 24 (twenty-four)

Page 25: Work

CONCEPTS: Work is part of living by the sea.

OBJECTIVE: I will know about life by the sea.

TEACHER GOAL: To teach the children what types of work people do by the sea.

READING INTEGRATION: main idea

VOCABULARY: boat, fishing pole, net, cooler

MATERIALS NEEDED: English walnut shells, toothpicks, clay, remnant pieces of construction paper, tape

TEACHING PAGE 25:

Write the vocabulary words on the board. Have the children listen as you read each word out loud. Read the words together. Discuss the meaning of each word.

Read the text aloud or ask a volunteer to read.

Discuss the picture.

Ask: Whose boat is this?
How is the boat used for work?
Can you find the nets?
Where is the place where the captain steers the boat?
What is the red, donut-shaped thing called? *(a lifesaver)*
What are the coolers used for? *(to hold the fish that are caught)*

WORK

Josh's dad uses a fishing boat to catch fish. There are fishing poles on the boat. There are big nets on the boat. There are coolers on the boat. Josh's dad puts fish in the coolers.

Josh helps clean his dad's fishing boat. Sometimes Josh gets to go out to sea with his dad to help catch fish.

page 25 (twenty-five)

ACTIVITY:

Boats! Boats!: Make walnut shell boats and sail them in buckets of water. All you need is a small piece of clay for the bottom of the shell, a toothpick, and a small upper sail. Mount the toothpick on the clay. Have the children design their own sails. Tape the sail to the toothpick.

Page 26 and 27:

CONCEPTS: Work is part of living by the sea.

OBJECTIVE: I will know about life by the sea.

TEACHER GOAL: To teach the children that lighthouses are part of life by the sea.

READING INTEGRATION: main idea

VOCABULARY: shine

MATERIALS NEEDED: pencils, Worksheet 18, crayons

TEACHING PAGES 26 AND 27:

Write the vocabulary word on the board. Point out the *sh* sound and the silent *e*. Ask if the *i* will be a long or short sound. Read the word together. Discuss its meaning.

Read the text on page 26. Show pictures of lighthouses.

    Ask: Where do you find lighthouses?
          When does the light shine?
          How would you get to the top of the lighthouse?

Read the directions on page 27. Go over each word choice. Read the statements one at a time. Allow children to circle the correct answers. Check answers as students complete the statements.

Other people work in lighthouses. Lighthouses are tall buildings. They shine a bright light into the sea. At night, ships can see this light. The light helps them find land. The light also warns the ships about sharp rocks ahead.

page 26 (twenty-six)

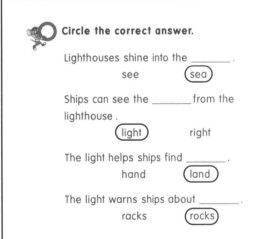

Circle the correct answer.

Lighthouses shine into the _____ .
    see   (sea)

Ships can see the _____ from the lighthouse .
    (light)   right

The light helps ships find _____ .
    hand   (land)

The light warns ships about _____ .
    racks   (rocks)

page 27 (twenty-seven)

Do Worksheet 18.

Before you begin:

1. Review what a compass means.
2. Point out the Key.
3. Discuss all symbols on the map. On the board put the following directions:

4 stones WEST	=	
1 stone NORTH	=	
3 stone SOUTH	=	
2 stones EAST	=	
3 stones NORTH	=	

Tell the class to circle and/or color the object next to the correct stone. Do one as an example to be sure the children understand:

    1 stone south = shovel and pail

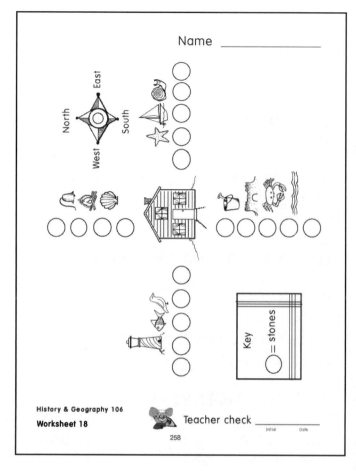

Name _____

History & Geography 106
Worksheet 18

258

Teacher check _____
Initial   Date

Page 28: Fun

CONCEPTS: Fun is part of living by the sea.

OBJECTIVE: I will know about life by the sea.

TEACHER GOAL: To teach children how people have fun by the sea.

READING INTEGRATION: main idea

VOCABULARY: beach, surf, sailboat

MATERIALS NEEDED: Worksheet 18, pencils, writing paper, scissors, construction paper, glue, sand, crayons or markers

TEACHING PAGE 28:

Write the vocabulary words on the board. Have the children listen as you read each word out loud. Ask volunteers to share the meaning of each word. Discuss meanings further if needed.

Read the text on page 28 aloud or ask a volunteer to read. Discuss the photograph. Ask the children what other things they can do at the beach *(build sand castles, draw pictures in the sand, collect shells, etc.)*

ACTIVITIES:

1. *Sand Paintings:* Supply the children with a piece of construction paper. Have them draw designs with glue, then sprinkle sand over the wet glue. Shake the excess sand off and decorate with details.

2. *Do Worksheet 19.*
Color the picture, then cut along the dotted lines in the picture. Cut out the sailboat. Allow children to sail their boats along the dotted line. Then have them write one or two sentences about their voyage and make a picture book telling about their sailboats.

FUN

Many people go to the beach to have fun. Josh enjoys swimming. Other people like to surf or ride in sailboats. Josh likes to watch the sailboats.

page 28 (twenty-eight)

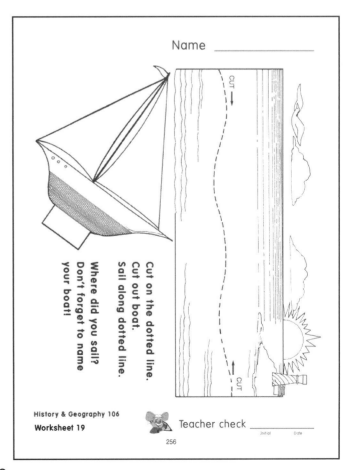

Name _____

Cut on the dotted line.
Cut out boat.
Sail along dotted line.

Where did you sail?
Don't forget to name
your boat!

History & Geography 106
Worksheet 19

256

Teacher check _____
Initial   Date

Page 29:

CONCEPTS: Fun is part of living by the sea.

OBJECTIVE: I will know about life by the sea.

TEACHER GOAL: To teach the children how people have fun by the sea.

READING INTEGRATION: main idea

VOCABULARY: seashell, collection

MATERIALS NEEDED: pencils, Worksheet 20, crayons, scissors, writing tablet

TEACHING PAGE 29:

1. Write out the vocabulary words on the board. Have the children listen as you read each word out loud.

2. Show the children examples of seashells. Tell them that there was once an animal living in each of the shells. Ask if they can think of other animals that live in shells (turtles, snails, etc.).

3. Discuss different collections that people have (stamps, dolls, etc.). Ask children to tell about collections they might have. Have a show and tell day where students can bring their collections to show the class.

4. Read the text on page 29. Allow time for the children to color the seashells.

ACTIVITIES:

1. *Writing tablet Exercise:* Have children copy the tongue twister: *"She sells seashells by the seashore."*

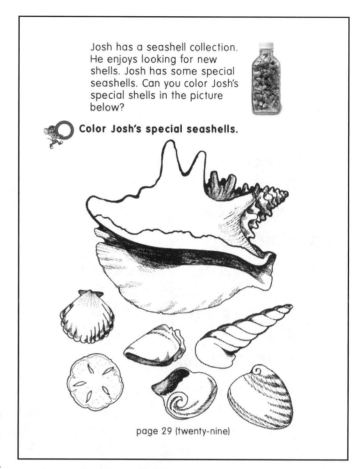

Josh has a seashell collection. He enjoys looking for new shells. Josh has some special seashells. Can you color Josh's special shells in the picture below?

Color Josh's special seashells.

page 29 (twenty-nine)

2. Creative Writing: As a class, write a story about the animal that once lived in one of the shells that is now on display in the classroom. Give the first line of the story and call on children to add one sentence at a time. Write the story on the board. Example: *"The little snail peeked out from his shell. He saw..."* Allow time for children to draw a picture to go with the story.

3. *Do Worksheet 20.* Ask volunteers to read the directions. Demonstrate how to cut the circle out of the shell. Allow students to complete the activity on their own.

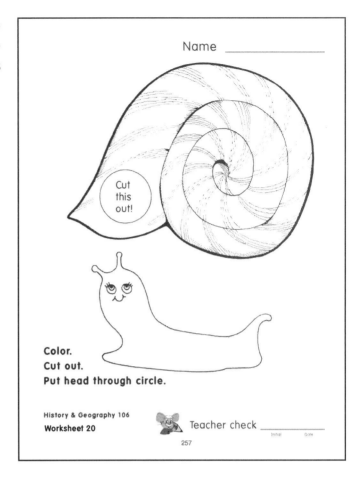

Name _____

Cut
this
out!

Color.
Cut out.
Put head through circle.

History & Geography 106
Worksheet 20

257

Teacher check _____
Initial   Date

Pages 30 and 31: Self Test 3

CONCEPTS: evaluation, categorizing

OBJECTIVE: I will know about life by the sea.

TEACHER GOAL: To check each child's progress.

BIBLE REFERENCES: Book of Jonah; Luke 5:1–11; Mark 6:47–52; Matthew 14:24–33; John 6:16–21.

READING INTEGRATION: following directions, recalling details

VOCABULARY: Review all vocabulary words.

MATERIALS NEEDED: pencils, Bible

TEACHING PAGES 30 AND 31:

Read all the directions and any words the children find difficult. Discuss the content of each picture.

Let the children do the pages independently.

Check at once. Review any concepts that were missed.

ACTIVITY:

1. *Sea Faith (stories from the Bible):* Many stories in the Bible refer to the sea and to God's people. Some stories the children would enjoy are these:

    a. Book of Jonah (Jonah and the whale). Have children do watercolor pictures of Jonah and the whale.

    b. Luke 5:1–11 (Jesus teaches the fishermen by the sea)

    c. Mark 6:47–52, Matthew 14:24–33; John 6:16–21 (Jesus stops a terrible storm on the sea)

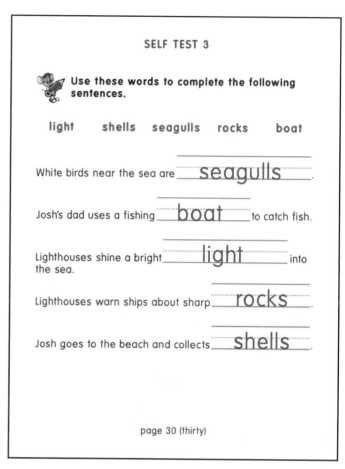

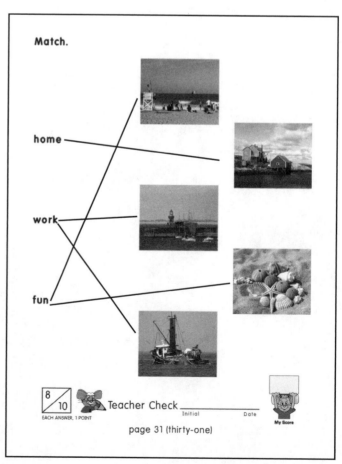

LIFEPAC Test and Alternate LIFEPAC Test:

Administer the test to the class as a group. Ask to have directions read or read them to the class. In either case, be sure that the children clearly understand. Put examples on the board if it seems necessary. Give ample time for each activity to be completed before going on to the next.

Correct immediately and discuss with the child. Review any concepts that have been missed. Give those children who do not achieve the 80% score additional copies of the worksheets and a list of vocabulary words to study. A parent or a classroom helper should help in the review.

When the child is ready, give the Alternate LIFEPAC Test. Use the same procedure as for the LIFEPAC Test.

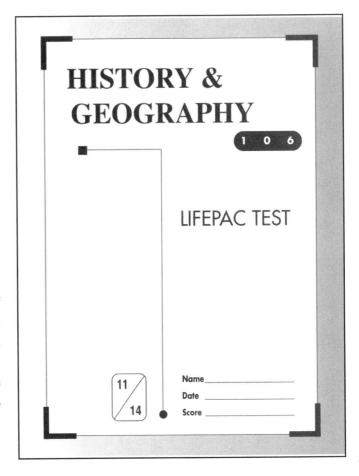

HISTORY & GEOGRAPHY

1 0 6

LIFEPAC TEST

11 / 14

Name _____

Date _____

Score _____

HISTORY & GEOGRAPHY 106: LIFEPAC TEST

EACH ANSWER, 1 POINT

Circle the correct answer.

_____ are used to plant seeds.
(Tractors)   Boats

Ships can see light from the _____ .
barn   (lighthouse)

Many cities have museums and _____ .
(zoos)   barns

_____ have houses, barns, and animals.
Cities   (Farms)

Many _____ can live in an apartment building.
animals   (families)

White birds that live near the ocean are called _____ .
(seagulls)   chickens

page 1 (one)

Use these words to complete the following sentences.

stores   boats   land   chores

A field is a large area of _____land_____ used to plant corn, beans, and oats.

Fishing _____boats_____ are used to catch fish.

Stanley, Lisa, and Josh all have _____chores_____ they must do every day.

Cities have houses, _____stores_____ , and fun things to do.

Match.

Farm

City

Sea

page 2 (two)

NOTES

page 3 (three)

LIFEPAC Test and Alternate LIFEPAC Test:

Administer the test to the class as a group. Ask to have directions read or read them to the class. In either case, be sure that the children clearly understand. Put examples on the board if it seems necessary. Give ample time for each activity to be completed before going on to the next.

Correct immediately and discuss with the child. Review any concepts that have been missed. Give those children who do not achieve the 80% score additional copies of the worksheets and a list of vocabulary words to study. A parent or a classroom helper should help in the review.

When the child is ready, give the Alternate LIFEPAC Test. Use the same procedure as for the LIFEPAC Test.

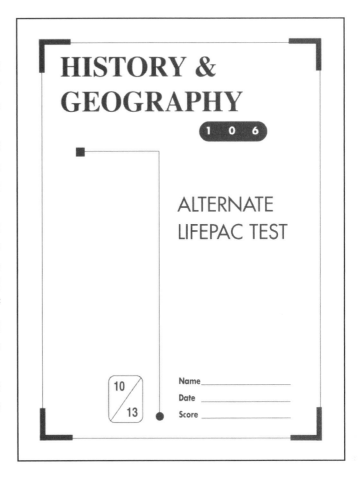

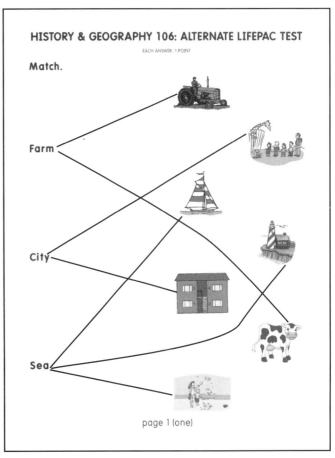

Alternate LIFEPAC Test (cont.)

Circle the picture that best completes each sentence.

Lisa will _____ .

Ships see light from the _____ .

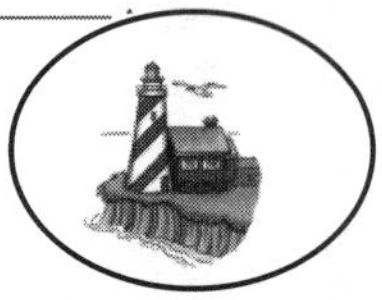

Use these words to complete the sentences.

shells   ball   chores   zoo

Children in the city like to go to the _____ zoo _____ .

Stanley likes to play _____ ball _____ with his family.

Josh collects _____ shells _____ .

Stanley, Lisa, and Josh all have to do _____ chores .

page 2 (two)

NOTES

page 3 (three)

Page 1: Community Helpers

CONCEPT: overall introduction to community helpers

OBJECTIVE: To introduce all the objectives

TEACHER GOAL: To teach the children the objectives of History & Geography 107.

BIBLE REFERENCE: Acts 2:44 through 47 and Acts 4:32 through 37

READING INTEGRATION: main idea, noting and recalling detail, speaking in a group, following oral directions, listening, writing a story

VOCABULARY: community, expects (special)

MATERIALS NEEDED: pictures of community helpers, writing tablet, drawing paper, pencils

COMMUNITY HELPERS

God gives you special helpers
to keep you safe.
Other helpers keep you well.
Some workers help you learn.
They all work together
for your community.

 Objectives

1. I can name some helpers God gives me.
2. I can tell how these helpers take care of me.
3. I can tell how God expects me to help these workers.

page 1 (one)

TEACHING PAGE 1:

Write the word community on the board. Say the word. Ask how many think they know what a community is. Talk about other words similar to community such as communion and communication. Emphasize that each of these words tells about something that people do together. Explain that a community is people living and working together. People in a community help each other in many ways. The stories in Acts 2:44 through 47 and Acts 4:32 through 37 are examples. What are some things people in a community cannot do alone? (put out fires, catch lawbreakers, make laws, practice medicine, and so on.)

Have the children open their books to page 1. Read the title. Talk about the helpers in the picture. Read the page together.

Ask the children to think of helpers who keep them safe, who keep them well, and who help them learn. Post community helper pictures on a bulletin board and label each one.

ACTIVITIES:

1. Write about a personal experience with any community helper.

2. Draw a picture about a personal experience with any community helper. Share these experiences with the whole class or in small sharing groups.

3. Arrange for a trip to the fire station or have a firefighter or police officer visit and talk to the children. At this time arrange for any other trips or classroom visitors for this unit, such as trips to the library or a hospital. You might ask a doctor, dentist, or nurse to speak to the children. A trip to city hall or other government buildings can be a real learning experience for your young future voters.

PART I: HELPERS WHO KEEP PEOPLE SAFE

Pages 2 and 3

CONCEPTS: helpers who keep people safe

OBJECTIVE: I can name some helpers God gives me.

TEACHER GOAL: To teach the children to tell about other duties that firemen have.

VOCABULARY: Policeman Bill, Fireman Dan, protect

MATERIALS NEEDED: pencils, crayons, scissors, glue, Worksheet 1, pictures (police, fireman, forest rangers, men and women in the armed forces, and so on), books about policemen and firemen, magazines, large drawing paper

TEACHING PAGE 2:

Write the words protect, fireman, and policeman on the board. Say the words. Talk about what each one means. Have the children give examples of ways the police and fire departments protect them. Use the word protect as often as possible in different situations during the school day. Point out that fireman and policeman are compound words.

Have the children open their books to page 2 and read the names under the pictures. Ask the children to share stories about any policemen or firemen they know personally. Read the page together.

TEACHING PAGE 3:

Remind the children that the icons indicate something they are to do.

Read the directions together. Make sure all the children know what to do. Be available to help those children who may not know all the words.

Read the directions for the second activity. After talking briefly about what

Policeman Bill　　　**Fireman Dan**

I. HELPERS WHO KEEP YOU SAFE

God gives you special helpers
to protect you.
You will meet Fireman Dan
and Policeman Bill.
You will learn how
you can help them.

page 2 (two)

policemen do for us, have the children complete the page.

ACTIVITIES:

1.　Begin work on a class scrapbook of community helpers. Supply magazines for pictures. Label each page and during the course of the unit have the children look for pictures of helpers to cut out and paste into the proper page.

2.　Instead of a class project, have each child make a scrapbook. Each page could have a picture of one helper and a story telling something about what that helper does.

3.　*Do Worksheet 1.*

Discuss what is happening in the picture. As children color the picture, ask them to think about other ways policemen and firemen help each other. This question would be good to ask a fireman or policeman in an interview.

Write <u>yes</u> **or** <u>no</u>.

Some helpers protect people.   yes

Your parents never need help.   no

All workers work together.   yes

Draw Policeman Bill helping someone.

page 3 (three)

Name _____

Talk about other ways policemen and firemen help each other.

History & Geography 107
Worksheet 1
with page 3

Teacher check _____
Initial   Date

Pages 4 and 5: Fireman Dan

CONCEPT: ways firemen protect people

OBJECTIVE: I can tell how these helpers take care of me.

TEACHER GOALS: To teach the children
    To tell what firemen do,
    To tell what they can do to help firemen, and
    To gain a sense of being a contributing member of the community.

READING INTEGRATION: main idea, noting and recalling details, drawing conclusions, speaking in front of a group, retelling in own words, listening, sequence, following written directions

VOCABULARY: checks, buildings, report, address (number, danger safe, telephone)

MATERIALS NEEDED: Worksheet 2, crayons, toy telephone, writing tablet, drawing paper, phone book, pencils

TEACHING PAGE 4:

Write the vocabulary words on the board, one at a time. Talk about each word and what it means. Review the list of words once more before having the children open their LIFEPACs to page 4. Discuss the picture on page 4 of the LIFEPAC. Talk about what Fireman Dan is doing. Ask the children to tell about other duties that firemen have besides putting out fires.

Read page 4 together. When the page has been read, talk about the ways we can help firemen to keep people safe. List the ways on the board or on chart paper. Keep this chart for future reference.

Pass out Worksheet 2. Give the children a few minutes to complete the dot-to-dots. Explain what is happening in each picture. Talk about the question in the discussion box.

MEET FIREMAN DAN

Fireman Dan helps put out fires.
He helps people who are in danger.
Fireman Dan checks buildings
to make sure they are safe.

Fireman Dan needs your help.
Learn how to report a fire.
Never play with fire.
Learn your own address and
telephone number.

page 4 (four)

Write 1, 2, 3 to show what happens first, second, and third.

Circle the pictures that show what a fireman does.

page 5 (five)

TEACHING PAGE 5:

Have the children turn to page 5 in their LIFEPACs. Read the directions to the first activity together. Talk briefly about what is happening in each picture. Tell the children to mark the pictures. Check the answers when everyone is finished. Have the children make any corrections with a crayon.

Read the directions to the second activity. Make sure the children understand the pictures. Check the activity as soon as all the children are finished.

ACTIVITIES:

1. Write several questions to ask the firemen when visiting the fire station.

2. Use a toy telephone to practice the correct way to phone in a fire report. Before using the phone, discuss and list the steps to be taken: (a) dial 911; (b) tell why you are calling fire or medical emergency; and (c) tell where the emergency is (give an address).

3. Using the list of ways to help firemen, have each child make a fire poster, including one or more rules of fire safety.

4. Read a book about firemen or fire safety.

5. Take a trip to a nearby fire station or arrange to have a fireman visit the class.

6. Write thank-you letters to the fire station.

Name _____

Fire Fighting of Long Ago

1776

1900

In what ways is firefighting today different from long ago?

History & Geography 107
Worksheet 2
with page 5

Teacher check _____
Initial   Date

71

Pages 6 and 7: Policeman Bill

CONCEPT: ways policeman protect people

OBJECTIVES:
I can tell how these helpers take care of me.
I can tell how God expects me to help these workers.

TEACHER GOALS: To teach the children
To tell some of the duties of policemen,
To tell some ways they can help policemen, and
To grow in their respect for and understanding of law enforcement officers.

BIBLE REFERENCE: Romans 13:1

READING INTEGRATION: main idea, following written directions, noting and recalling details, dramatization, retelling in own words, writing sentences

VOCABULARY: direct, arresting, law, strangers (traffic, sick, break, obey, signs)

MATERIALS NEEDED: writing tablet, pencils, crayons, flashcards of traffic signs from Social Studies 102.

TEACHING PAGE 6:
Introduce the new words. Write them on the board and talk about their meanings.
Have the children open their LIFEPACs to page 6. Discuss the picture. In the reading and discussion of this entire page, policemen should be spoken of with great respect. The children hear so many negative things about policemen in the secular world, that the building of a positive image of these men should be a vital concern of the Christian school. Introduce this lesson by reading Romans 13:1 to the class and discuss who are the authorities it refers to.

MEET POLICEMAN BILL

Policeman Bill is your friend.
He helps you if you get lost.
Sometimes he directs traffic.
Policeman Bill helps people
who are hurt or sick.
He helps you by arresting
people who break the law.

Policeman Bill needs your help.
Always obey traffic signs.
Never take candy or rides
from strangers.
Learn to ride a bike safely.
Look both ways
before crossing a street.

page 6 (six)

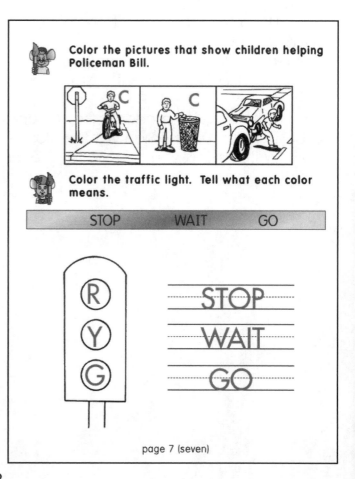

Color the pictures that show children helping Policeman Bill.

Color the traffic light. Tell what each color means.

STOP   WAIT   GO

R
Y
G

STOP
WAIT
GO

page 7 (seven)

Read page 6 together. Discuss more ways policemen help people and ways that the children can help them.

TEACHING PAGE 7:

Read the directions together and make sure the children understand each picture. Before completing the second activity, review some common traffic signs, especially the stop light. Review the location of each color and what it means. Check the page as soon as all the children are finished.

ACTIVITIES:

1. Invite a police officer to visit the class and talk to the children.

2. Individually or in groups, have the children prepare questions to ask when the police officer visits.

3. Act out situations in which policeman Bill helps people. Involve as many children as possible. Girls as well as boys should play the part of the police officer.

4. In small groups have the children share what they learned when the police officer visited the classroom.

5. Write letters thanking the police officer for visiting the class.

Pages 8 and 9: Activity Pages

MATERIALS NEEDED: crayons, pencils, Worksheet 3, toy telephone, free materials of U.S. Department of Agriculture: Forest-Service

TEACHING PAGES 8 and 9:

Write all the vocabulary words from part one on the board. Give a definition for one of the words. Have the children tell which word you defined.

An alternative to this activity is to ask the children to open their LIFEPAC to page 4 and, find the word that tells about where you live and circle it with a pencil. Then ask one child to read the word he has circled. Continue in the same way with the other vocabulary words.

Have the children open their LIFEPACs to pages 8 and 9. Read all directions together. The picture may be any part of town a child wishes to portray. Write the name of your community on the board for the children to copy. Make sure the children understand all directions and pictures.

Check page 9 as soon as all the children are finished.

ACTIVITIES:

1. Have the children share their pictures on page 8 with either the whole class or a small sharing group.

2. *Do Worksheet 3.*

Pass out the Worksheet. Discuss the picture. Talk about what forest rangers do to protect people and wildlife. Talk about the difference between forest and brush fires and building fires. Have materials available from the Forest Service. Have the children list ways they can help the forest rangers.

3. Have the children draw pictures of ways they can help protect our forests and wildlife.

4. Give the children a chance to pantomime different jobs of firemen and police officers. Have the rest of the class try to guess what they are doing.

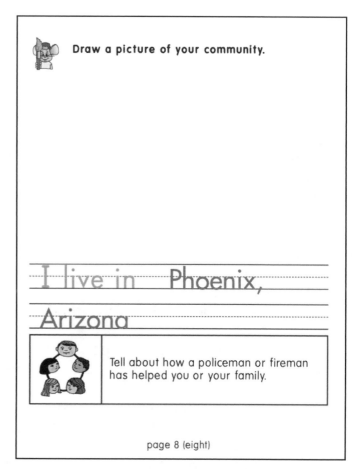

page 8 (eight)

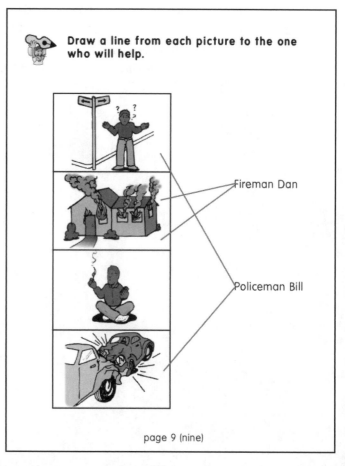

page 9 (nine)

Name _____

Forest rangers are policemen **and** firemen. They protect people and wildlife.

History & Geography 107
Worksheet 3
with page 9

Teacher check _____
                 Initial   Date

Page 10: Self Test 1

CONCEPT: helpers who keep us safe

OBJECTIVES:
   I can name some helpers God gives me.
   I can tell how these helpers take care of me.
   I can tell how God expects me to help these workers.

TEACHER GOAL: evaluation of section one

READING INTEGRATION: following written directions, recalling details

VOCABULARY: Review all the vocabulary.

MATERIALS NEEDED: pencils, vocabulary flashcards

TEACHING PAGE 10:
   Go over the word cards several times. The children should know these words.
   Have the class open their LIFEPACs to page 10. Tell them they will do this page by themselves in order to find out how much they remember about firemen and police officers. Make sure the children understand the directions and any illustrations. Give them plenty of time to complete the page independently. Be available to help those who have a problem.
   Check the page with the class. Errors should be explained immediately and corrections made with a crayon or colored pencil. Most children are able to check and correct their own self tests.

SELF TEST 1

Write yes or no.

Policeman Bill puts out fires. __no__

Fireman Dan is your friend. __yes__

A red light tells you to go. __no__

Never take a ride from a stranger. __yes__

Policemen and fireman help people who are hurt. __yes__

Circle the picture that shows how you can help a policeman.

5/6   Teacher Check _____ Initial ___ Date
page 10 (ten)

ACTIVITIES:
   1.   Work on community helpers scrapbook.
   2.   Make a safety collage. Bring out the magazines. Pass out 9" x 12" white drawing paper. Have the children look for pictures showing safe ways of doing things. Paste these pictures randomly all over the drawing paper.
   3.   Read books on safety and discuss them with the class.

PART II: PEOPLE WHO HELP YOU STAY WELL

Page 11

CONCEPT: people who help others stay well

OBJECTIVE: I can name some helpers God gives me.

TEACHER GOALS: To teach the children
To consider the importance of workers who help them stay well, and
To name four health workers.

READING INTEGRATION: main idea, noting and recalling details, following written directions, speaking in a group, listening, drawing conclusions

VOCABULARY: nurse, doctor, dentist, city worker

MATERIALS NEEDED: pictures of community health workers, scrapbook materials, pencils, crayons

TEACHING PAGE 11:
Have the children open their books to page 11. Talk briefly about each picture. A few children may want to share a personal experience.
Read page 11 together. Tell the children to draw their own face in the empty circle at the top. As they work, talk about how they can help themselves and others stay well. After checking the first activity, have the children finish the page.

ACTIVITIES:
1. Work on community helpers scrapbooks.
2. Arrange for doctor and/or dentist to visit the class.

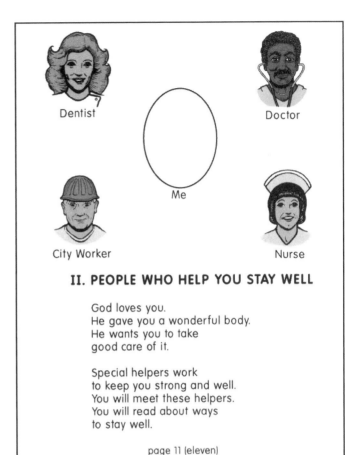

Dentist

Doctor

City Worker

Me

Nurse

II. PEOPLE WHO HELP YOU STAY WELL

God loves you.
He gave you a wonderful body.
He wants you to take
good care of it.

Special helpers work
to keep you strong and well.
You will meet these helpers.
You will read about ways
to stay well.

page 11 (eleven)

Pages 12 and 13: Dr. Jones

CONCEPT: why we need doctors and nurses

OBJECTIVES:
    I can tell how these helpers take care of me.
    I can tell how God expects me to help these workers.

TEACHER GOALS: To teach the children
    To tell about the work of doctors and nurses, and
    To understand that God gives us doctors, nurses, and medicine.

READING INTEGRATION: main idea, noting and recalling details, dramatization, following written directions, drawing conclusions, listening, writing a story

VOCABULARY: ears, throat, breathe, medicine, exercise (weather, eyes, listens)

MATERIALS NEEDED: Worksheet 4, writing tablet, pencils

TEACHING PAGES 12 and 13:
    Before reading the page, show pictures of doctors and nurses. Discuss what is taking place in each picture. Talk about the children's own experiences with doctors and nurses.
    Have the children open their LIFEPACs to pages 12 and 13. Read the pages together. Discuss other things a doctor and nurse do. Stress that doctors are our helpers provided by God to help us when we are sick. Have the children name more ways they can help their doctor.
    Read the activity directions on page 13 and let the children answer the questions independently. Identify any illustration they do not recognize.

MEET DOCTOR JONES

Doctor Jones helps you
when you are sick or hurt.
He checks your ears, eyes,
and throat.
He listens to you breathe.
He might give you medicine.
God helps him know
what is best for you.

Miss Day is a nurse.
She works with Doctor Jones.
Miss Day and Doctor Jones are
your friends.

page 12 (twelve)

You can help your doctor.
Eat foods that are good for you.
Get plenty of exercise.
Dress right for the weather.
Take your medicine
when you are sick.
Never play with medicine.

 Circle the picture that answers each question.

Who helps Doctor Jones?

What helps you stay well?

What does a doctor use to listen to you breathe?

page 13 (thirteen)

ACTIVITIES:

1. *Do Worksheet 4.*

Read the directions together and let the children work the page independently. Talk about each picture as you check the page.

2. Read books on what to do in common emergencies such as a person choking or getting a bee sting and discuss them with the class.

3. Have the children write a story about their trip to the doctor.

4. Make up a list of questions to ask the doctor when he visits the class.

Pages 14 and 15: Doctor Brooks

CONCEPT: why we need dentists

OBJECTIVES:
I can tell how these helpers take care of me.
I can tell how God expects me to help these workers.

TEACHER GOALS: To teach the children
To tell something a dentist does,
To tell how they can help their dentist, and
To understand the importance of caring for their teeth.

READING INTEGRATION: main idea, noting and recalling detail, following oral and written directions.

VOCABULARY: teeth, strong, healthy, cavities, brush, chart, month (cleans)

MATERIALS NEEDED: large drawing paper, crayons

TEACHING PAGES 14 and 15:

Write the new words on the board. Talk about each word and what it means.

Before reading, ask the children what they think a dentist does and how they can help a dentist care for teeth. Write these suggestions on the board.

Read pages 14 and 15 together, comparing the things the children said with the text, especially the things they can do to help the dentist.

Collect some pamphlets about dental hygiene and show them to the class. Explain that the lady who helps the dentist is called a dental technician and that a dentist who only helps people get straight teeth is called an orthodontist. Dentists today do many things. They all work to keep children's teeth in good shape.

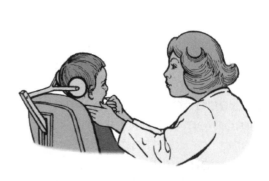

MEET DOCTOR BROOKS

Doctor Brooks is a dentist.
She helps you take care
of your teeth.
Strong, healthy teeth mean
a strong, healthy body.
Doctor Brooks cleans teeth and
looks for cavities.
She will fill any cavities.

page 14 (fourteen)

You can help your dentist.
Brush your teeth often.
Eat foods that build strong teeth.
Have six-month check-ups.

 Keep this chart for one week.

**I BRUSHED MY TEETH
THIS MORNING**

Sunday	X
Monday	X
Tuesday	X
Wednesday	X
Thursday	X
Friday	X
Saturday	X

page 15 (fifteen)

One of the most important ways the children can help the dentist is by regular cleaning of their teeth. Many times the children will hurry off to school in the morning without brushing. Explain the chart on page 15. Demonstrate the right way to brush teeth. Check the charts every day of the week.

ACTIVITIES:

1. Visit a dentist's office.
2. Set up a dentist's office and/or doctor's office and allow the children to act out various situations. Roles would include doctor, dentist, nurse, technician, receptionist, and patients.

Pages 16 and 17: Mr. James

CONCEPT: City workers help keep communities clean

OBJECTIVES:
I can tell how these helpers take care of me.
I can tell how God expects me to help these workers.

TEACHER GOALS: To teach the children
To tell about city workers who help keep cities clean and healthy,
To tell how they can help keep their community clean, and
To understand the importance of keeping their community clean.

READING INTEGRATION: main idea, noting and recalling details, predicting outcomes

VOCABULARY: litter bug, trash

MATERIALS NEEDED: Worksheet 5, drawing paper, paper sacks, construction paper (all colors), tempera paint or crayons, glue, pencils

TEACHING 16 and 17:
Write the vocabulary words on the board. Say them as you point to them.
Ask the children to tell what each one means.
Have the children open their LIFEPACs to page 16. Talk about what they see in the picture. Ask the children to tell how the garbage is taken care of where they live. List other city workers who are involved in keeping the city clean. The list might include street sweeper operators, tractor operators at city dumps, health inspectors, and so on.

MEET MR. JAMES

Mr. James is a city worker.
He drives a big truck.
He helps keep your
community clean.
He helps make it
a healthy place to live.
You can help keep your
community clean.
Don't be a litter-bug.
Always use trash cans.

page 16 (sixteen)

Follow the dots.

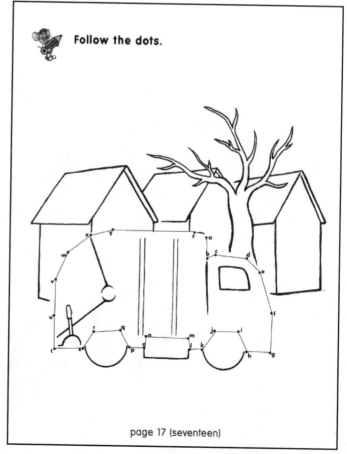

page 17 (seventeen)

Read the page together. Have the children think of and list other ways to help keep the city clean. This list might include a school-ground cleanup and a neighborhood or park cleanup program.

Give the children time to do the dot-to-dot on page 17. Have them color the picture.

ACTIVITIES:

1. *Do Worksheet 5.*
Tell the children to decide what is happening in the first picture in each row. Then have them circle the picture on the right that best shows what will happen next. Check and discuss it together.

2. Organize a clean-up program around school or in the neighborhood. Give the children paper sacks to fill with litter on their walk around the school grounds or through the neighborhood.

3. *Art Project*: Using torn construction paper shapes, have each child construct a two dimensional litter bug. Have them use this "bug" as part of a poster reminding people not to be litter bugs. The poster itself can be done on heavy white paper with tempera paints or crayons. Paste the litter bug into the picture in the appropriate place.

Pages 18 and 19: Activity Pages

VOCABULARY: paramedics

MATERIALS NEEDED: pencils, crayons, tempera paint (black and other colors), white drawing paper, 1" x 1" pieces of sponge, writing tablet, Worksheet 6, vocabulary cards for section two of the LIFEPAC

TEACHING PAGE 18:

If the children know their vocabulary words, they should have no difficulty completing page 18. Read all directions together. Identify the illustrations. Allow enough time for all the children to finish the picture.

Check the page as soon as everyone is finished. Help should be given to children with any errors. The errors should be corrected by the student with a crayon.

TEACHING PAGE 19:

Have the children turn to page 19. If the children visited the fire station, they most likely saw a rescue unit. It may not have looked just like the one in the picture, though. The children may have experiences related to paramedics and rescue work that they would like to share as they color this page. Talk about what they remember being told while at the fire station.

ACTIVITIES:

1.   *Do Worksheet 6.*
This sheet will help you to know if any vocabulary words are not easily recognized. Identify all pictures before the children begin. Check together and discuss as a review page.

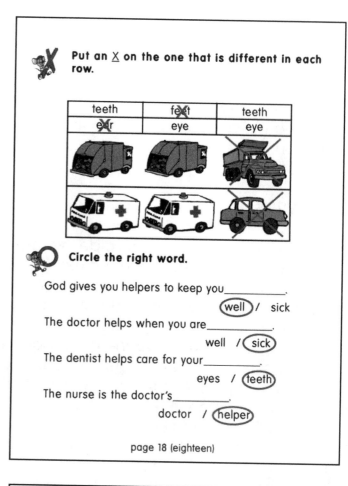

Put an X on the one that is different in each row.

teeth	feet	teeth
ear	eye	eye

Circle the right word.

God gives you helpers to keep you_____.
well / sick

The doctor helps when you are_____.
well / sick

The dentist helps care for your_____.
eyes / teeth

The nurse is the doctor's_____.
doctor / helper

page 18 (eighteen)

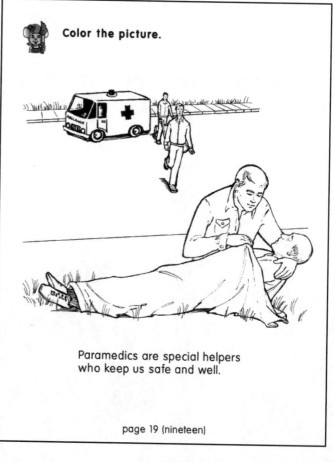

Color the picture.

Paramedics are special helpers who keep us safe and well.

page 19 (nineteen)

2. Use flashcards to review all vocabulary words for section two. Check the page as soon as everyone is finished.

3. *Art Project:* Pass out large 12" x 18" white or blue construction paper. Tell the children they are going to paint a city truck, street equipment, fire trucks, rescue squad, ambulance, or police car. Make the outline of the vehicle with heavy black crayon or tempera paint. The picture will be "colored" by patting a sponge piece dipped in paint wherever that color is desired. Change sponges when changing color. Two or three color choices should be sufficient. Use the completed pictures for a very colorful bulletin board display.

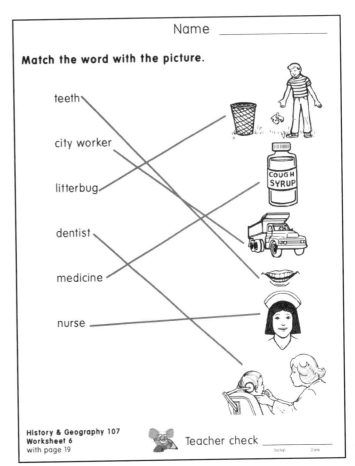

Name _____

Match the word with the picture.

teeth

city worker

litterbug

dentist

medicine

nurse

History & Geography 107
Worksheet 6
with page 19

Teacher check _____
Initial   Date

Page 20: Activity Page

MATERIALS NEEDED: pencils, crayons

TEACHING PAGE 20:

Read the directions to the children. Have them do the page independently.

Check it together. Discuss the answers and the drawings as a review for the self test.

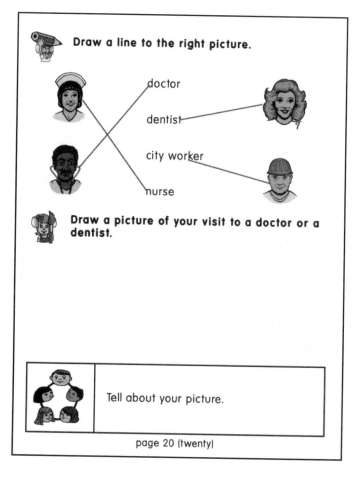

Page 21: Self Test 2

CONCEPT: evaluation of workers who keep us well

OBJECTIVES:
I can name some helpers God gives me.
I can tell how these helpers take care of me.
I can tell how God expects me to help these workers.

TEACHER GOAL: To evaluate the children's comprehension of section two.

READING INTEGRATION: following written directions, sequence, recalling details

VOCABULARY: Review all the vocabulary.

MATERIALS NEEDED: writing tablet, pencils, scrapbook materials

TEACHING PAGE 21:
Have the children open their LIFEPAC to page 21. Read the directions together. Identify all the illustrations. The children should finish the page independently.

As soon as all the children are finished, check the page together. If there were any serious errors on the part of any student, this is the time to clear them up. Have the children correct their pages with a crayon. The teacher should walk around the room while the pages are being checked.

ACTIVITY:
1. Work on community helpers scrapbook. Find pictures of helpers who keep us well. Write stories about one or more of the helpers.

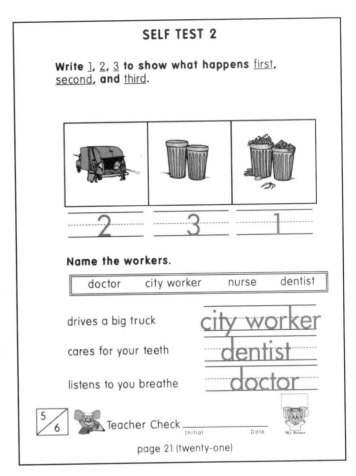

PART III: FRIENDS WHO HELP US LEARN

PAGES 22 and 23

CONCEPT: friends who help us learn.

OBJECTIVE: I can name some helpers God gives me.

TEACHER GOALS: To teach the children
To recognize people who help them learn, and
To name three people who help them learn

READING INTEGRATION: main idea, noting and recalling details, following written directions

VOCABULARY: librarian (minister, teacher)

MATERIALS NEEDED: writing tablet, pencils, crayons

TEACHING PAGES 22 and 23:

Have the children turn to page 22. Use the pictures and labels to introduce the vocabulary words.

Read the page together. As they read the sentence about each helper, ask what other things that person teaches besides what is written in the LIFEPAC.

After the discussion, look at the first activity on page 23. Read the directions and let the children match the faces and names. Encourage them to look at page 22 if they need help.

Follow the same procedure with the second activity. Read the directions together. Check the page together when everyone is finished.

ACTIVITIES:

1. Arrange to visit the library sometime in the next few weeks.

2. Have the children list as many people as they can think of who helps them learn.

minister

teacher

librarian

III. FRIENDS WHO HELP YOU LEARN

You learn many things.
Your minister teaches you
about God's love.
Your teacher helps you learn
to read and write.
The librarian helps you
learn about books.

page 22 (twenty-two)

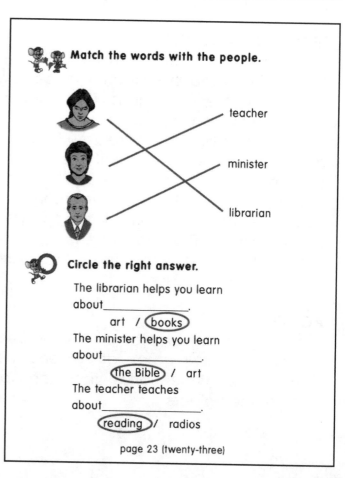

Match the words with the people.

teacher

minister

librarian

Circle the right answer.

The librarian helps you learn about_____.
art / (books)

The minister helps you learn about_____.
(the Bible) / art

The teacher teaches about_____.
(reading) / radios

page 23 (twenty-three)

3. Write one or two sentences about each of the three helpers on page 2 in the writing tablet. Have the children tell what they have learned from each one.

4. Tell about a favorite book.

5. Arrange to have a minister visit the class and talk about what he does.

Pages 24 and 25: Ministers

CONCEPT: all about the minister

OBJECTIVE:
I can tell how these helpers take care of me.
I can tell how God expects me to help these workers.

TEACHER GOALS: To teach the children
To understand that their minister is a good friend and someone to know and respect, and
To tell something they can do for their minister.

READING INTEGRATION: main idea, noting and recalling details, following directions, drawing conclusions, listening, retelling in own words

VOCABULARY: baptizes (pray, church)

MATERIALS NEEDED: pictures of ministers showing different ways they dress, pictures of churches, pencils, writing tablet, crayons or paint

TEACHING PAGES 24 and 25:
Find out how many of the children know the name of their own pastor. This information is probably in the school record if you need to help them out. Those children who have no church home might consider the school pastor as their pastor. Ask the children to share what they think pastors do.
Have them turn to page 24 in their LIFEPACs and read the page to themselves. After all have finished reading, let the children share what they read. Talk about what pastors really do besides what they read in the LIFEPAC. If you have invited a pastor to speak to the class, make a list of some questions the children would like him to answer.

MEET YOUR MINISTER

Your minister is your friend.
He is God's helper.
He tells how Jesus came
to save all people from their sins.
Christians are part of God's family.

You can help your minister.
Pray for him every day.
Pray for your church, too.

page 24 (twenty-four)

Write the answer on the line.

The minister is your ___friend___.
find / friend

Jesus came to save ___all___ people.
many / all

___Pray___ for your minister.
Help / Pray

Circle the picture that goes with each helper.

page 25 (twenty-five)

The children should turn to page 25. Read all the directions together. Have the children complete the page independently. Check the page with the class when everyone is finished.

ACTIVITIES:

1. Write a prayer for your pastor and your church. Before the children begin, discuss the kinds of requests a person might make concerning the pastor and the church.

2. Show the pictures of different pastors and churches. Talk about how the children's churches differ from the ones in the picture.

3. Have the child draw and color or paint their own church, either an inside or outside view. They should include the pastor in the picture.

Pages 26 and 27: Teachers

CONCEPT: all about teachers
OBJECTIVES:

I can tell how these helpers take care of me.

I can tell how God expects me to help these workers.

TEACHER GOAL: To teach the children to be aware that teachers do more than just teach school.

READING INTEGRATION: main idea, noting and recalling details, following written directions, writing a two paragraph story, speaking in a group, listening

VOCABULARY: math (write, teacher, listen)

MATERIALS NEEDED: writing tablet, pencils, crayons, scrapbooks, glue, scissors, magazines

TEACHING PAGES 26 and 27:

Have the children open their LIFEPACs to page 26. Ask someone to tell who they see in the picture. Read the page together. List on the board all the things learned during the day. This list should be the children's list. Then make a list of all the things the children think they should do for the teacher. All together, evaluate the lists. Help the children decide if the lists are complete or if anything was missed. Read the directions on page 27. As the children finish their pictures have some of them share their pictures and ideas with the whole class.

ACTIVITIES:

1. Have each child write a prayer asking God to help them do their best in school and to remember to help the teacher.
2. Have the children write a story in their writing tablets entitled "If I Were a Teacher". Some of these may be shared with the class.

MEET YOUR TEACHER

You will learn to read and write.
You will learn to do math.

Your teacher helps you learn.
She is God's helper.
God wants you to learn.

Your teacher needs your help.
Listen to her.
Do your work.
Pray for your teacher every day.

page 26 (twenty-six)

 Draw a picture of something you can do for your teacher and your minister.

 Talk about your picture.
Carry out your plan.

page 27 (twenty-seven)

3. Work on community helpers scrapbooks.

Pages 28 and 29: Librarians

CONCEPT: all about the librarian

OBJECTIVES:

I can tell how these helpers take care of me.

I can tell how God expects me to help these workers.

TEACHER GOALS: To teach the children

To visit the library, and

To respect the librarian and treat the books as their own.

READING INTEGRATION: main idea, noting and recalling details, sequence, speaking in a group, listening, following written direction, fact/ fantasy.

VOCABULARY: library, librarian, card, buys, return (careful)

MATERIALS NEEDED: Worksheet 7, pencils, drawing paper, writing tablet, thread, construction paper, clothes hangers or dowels

TEACHING PAGES 28 and 29:

Write the vocabulary words on the board. Read each one and explain what it means. Have the children turn to page 28 in their LIFEPACs.

Read page 28 together. Discuss what was read. Talk about what the children have observed on their own trips to the library. What did they see the librarian doing?

Read page 29 together. Have the children think of some other ways they can help the librarian.

Read the directions for the activity on page 29. It might be necessary to identify the illustrations before the children begin working. When all the children have completed the activity, check it together. It

MEET YOUR LIBRARIAN

Have you been to a library?
The librarian works
at the library.
She helps you get
a library card.
She shows you how
to find books.
The librarian buys books
for the library.

page 28 (twenty-eight)

You can help the librarian.
Always have clean hands.
Be careful with library books.
Keep your library books
in a safe place.
Return your books on time.

Write 1, 2, 3 to show what happens first, second, and third.

page 29 (twenty-nine)

might be necessary to identify the illustrations before the children begin working.

ACTIVITIES:

1. Review the concept of fact versus fantasy. Pass out Worksheet 7. Tell the children they are to decide whether each book pictured is fact or fantasy. They are to circle the correct word. Check the page together. Talk about any stories that the children are not sure about.

2. *Art Project:* Have each child pick a favorite Bible story. Draw and cut out all the most important characters in the story. Tie thread through each character and hang them from a hanger or dowel. Suspend the mobiles all around the room.

3. Write original stories. These stories could be compiled and duplicated. This book of original stories could then be sent home with each child.

4. Write or tell about a favorite book. This may be a small group activity. Have the children draw pictures to illustrate their talk.

5. Review the vocabulary words for section three.

Name _____

Tell if the book is fact or fantasy.

ALL ABOUT TRUCKS	Three Billy Goats Gruff
(fact) fantasy	fact (fantasy)
LIFEPAC Community Helper	Holy Bible
(fact) fantasy	(fact) fantasy
Winnie-the-pooh	CINDERELLA
fact (fantasy)	fact (fantasy)

History & Geography 107
Worksheet 7
with page 29

Teacher check _____
Initial   Date

Pages 30 and 31: Activity Pages

MATERIALS NEEDED: crayons, writing tablet

TEACHING PAGES 30 and 31:

Discuss the picture on page 31 carefully before the children color the picture.

Read the direction on page 31. After the children finish their drawing, have them write three paragraphs about the book in their writing tablets.

Allow class time for the children to read their paragraphs and discuss their pictures. Remind them of the proper speaking rules they have learned in Language Arts.

Color this picture.

page 30 (thirty)

Draw a picture about your favorite library book.

Tell about this book you have read.

page 31 (thirty-one)

Page 32: Self Test 3

CONCEPT: friends who help us learn

OBJECTIVES:

I can name some helpers God gives me.
I can tell how these helpers take care of me.
I can tell how God expects me to help these workers.

TEACHER GOAL: To evaluate section three and determine whether the children are ready for the LIFEPAC Test.

READING INTEGRATION: following written directions, recalling details

MATERIALS NEEDED: pencils, scrapbook, magazines, glue, scissors

TEACHING PAGE 32:

Have the children open their LIFEPAC to page 32. Read the directions together. Identify all the illustrations. The children should finish the page independently.

As soon as all the children are finished, check the page together. If there were any serious errors on the part of any student, this is the time to clear them up. Have the children correct their pages with a crayon. The teacher should walk around the room while the pages are being checked.

ACTIVITY:

Have the children finish the community helpers scrapbooks. These can be sent home along with page 33 from the LIFEPAC.

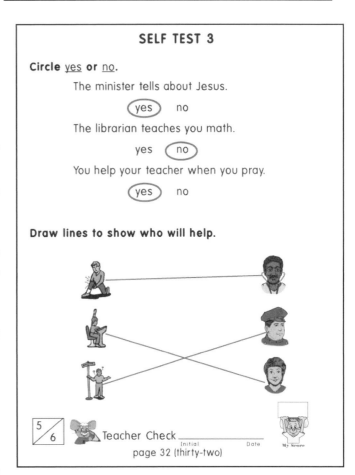

Page 33: Take Home Activity Page

MATERIALS NEEDED: crayons

TEACHING PAGE 33:

Read the directions and explain the color key.

Let the children do the page independently or take it home to do.

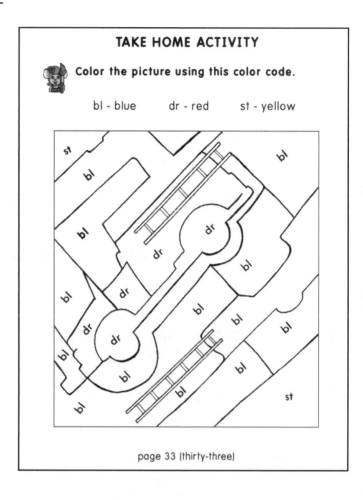

LIFEPAC TEST AND ALTERNATE LIFEPAC TEST

Administer the test to the class as a group. Ask to have directions read or read them to the class. In either case, be sure that the children clearly understand. Put examples on the board if it seems necessary. Give ample time for each activity to be completed before going to the next.

Correct immediately and discuss with the child.

Review any concepts that have been missed.

Give those children who do not achieve the 80% score additional copies of the worksheets and a list of vocabulary words to study. A parent or a classroom helper should help in the review.

When the child is ready, give the Alternate LIFEPAC Test. Use the same procedure as for the LIFEPAC TEST.

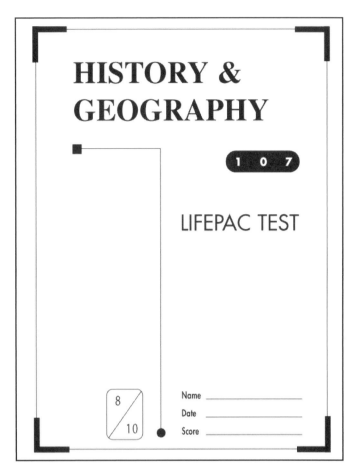

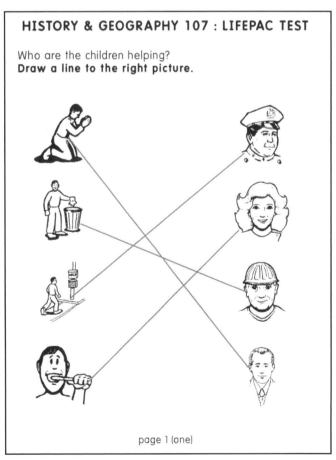

Circle the picture that goes with each helper.

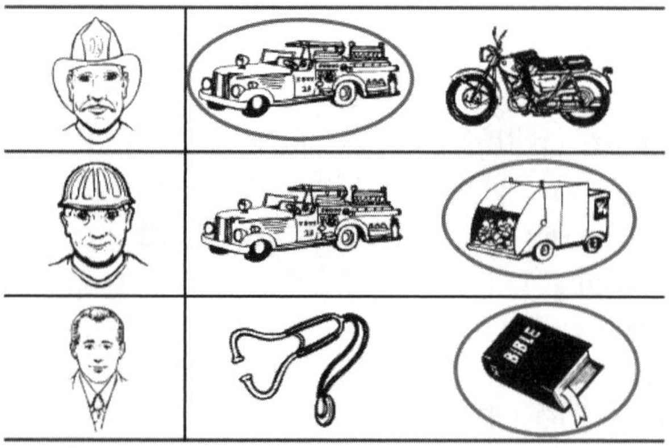

Circle the right answer.

God gives you special _____.

(helpers) / here

We help the dentist when we brush our _____.

hair / (teeth)

We help Fireman Dan when we are careful
with _____.

bikes / (fire)

page 2 (two)

NOTES

page 3 (three)

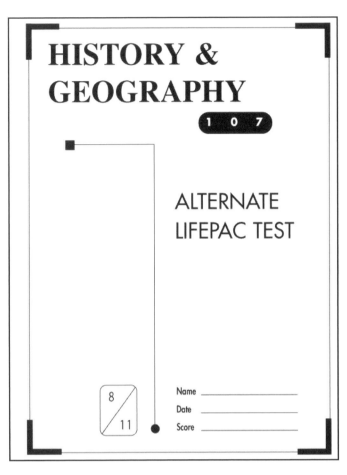

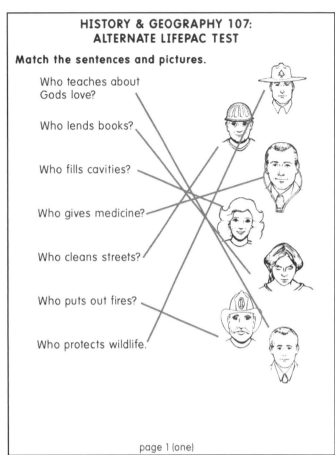

Page 1: I Love My Country

CONCEPT: I love my country.

OBJECTIVE: To introduce all of the objectives

TEACHER GOALS: To teach the children
To understand a table of contents, and
To understand the difference between a state and a country.

READING INTEGRATION: table of contents, main idea, noting and recalling details, syllables, compound words

VOCABULARY: United States, America, President, pledge, allegiance (laws, rules, country)

MATERIALS NEEDED: large maps of the world and the United States, globe, pocket chart, vocabulary cards and vocabulary definition cards, writing tablet

TEACHING PAGE 1:

Pass out the new LIFEPAC. Read the name of the LIFEPAC. Have the children open to the contents. *Ask the following questions:*
"Who can tell what a contents page is?"
"How many sections are in this LIFEPAC?"
"Who can find a compound word on the page?"
"Who can find and read the two names of people on this page?"
"On what page will you read about our first President? the flag? Christopher Columbus?"
"What are holidays?"
Have the children turn to page 1. Put up the two large maps on the board where everyone can see them. Ask the children to point to the map that is like the one on page 1. Tell them the name *United States* as you write it on the board. Then ask in what state the children live. Have them find it on the wall map and then put an *X* on it on the LIFEPAC map.

I LOVE MY COUNTRY

Pilgrims landed here.

You live in a free country.
It is called the United States of America.
Your country is over 200 years old.
The United States was built
on God's laws.

Objectives

1. I can tell the name of my country.
2. I can tell how my country began.
3. I can name our first President.
4. I can tell why people need rules.
5. I can say the Pledge of Allegiance.

page 1 (one)

Explain to the children that when our country first began a long time ago, it was very small. Point to the darkened eastern states. Ask the children to count the states. Use the wall map to compare. Rhode Island is not distinguishable on the LIFEPAC map. Tell the class that in 200 years our country has grown from 13 states to 50 states. Using the world map, draw a line around the continental U.S. plus Alaska and Hawaii. Have several children find the United States on the globe.

Read page 1 together. As the children read objective one, reiterate the name of the country. Often times small children have a difficult time remembering the difference between a country, a state, and a city.

ACTIVITIES:

1. Have the children write a sentence in their writing tablets about where they live.

Example:

I live in the United States of America. Using the world map, help the children to see that the United States is just one country in America.

2. Tell the children they are going to match some cards with their new words on them and cards that tell what the new words mean.

Put all the vocabulary cards into a column on the left side of the pocket chart. Say the words as you place the cards. Have the children read the words. Hold up the definitions one at a time. Read the definition card with the class. Now ask one child to come up and put the definition in the pocket next to the word it tells about. Do the others word cards the same way.

PART I: HOW AMERICA WAS DISCOVERED

Pages 2 and 3

CONCEPT: the discovery of America

OBJECTIVE: I can tell how my country began.

TEACHER GOAL: To help the children to gain some understanding of the early history of our country.

READING INTEGRATION: main idea, noting and recalling details, following written directions, speaking in a group, listening, syllables

VOCABULARY: discovered, Indians, (ocean)

MATERIALS NEEDED: world map; globe; pictures of sailing vessels, circa 1492; pencils; crayons

TEACHING PAGE 2 and 3:

Write the word *discover* on the board. Talk about what it means. Encourage the children to share personal experiences of discovering things. As each child shares, ask if he made the discovery on purpose or by accident.

Have the children open their LIFEPACs to page 2 and read the title. Explain that the discovery of America was really an accident. None of the first Europeans who came here had known in advance that a new country was on the other side of the ocean. Some of these men were looking for other countries when they discovered America.

Read page 2 together. Briefly, talk about several early explorers who came to America. Leif Ericson explored the Canadian coastline in the area of Nova Scotia; Amerigo Vespucci, after whom our continent was named, explored the coastline from Florida to the Delaware or

I. HOW AMERICA WAS DISCOVERED

For a long time
only Indians lived in our country.
Then other men came
across the ocean.
They sailed in small ships.
These men found a new land.
More and more people came
to live in this new land.

page 2 (two)

 Circle <u>yes</u> or <u>no</u>.

The United States is 100 years old.

yes (no)

You live in the United States.

(yes) no

 Color the picture.

 What is Columbus doing in this picture?

page 3 (three)

Chesapeake Bay; and Columbus, whose explorations were limited to the islands of the Caribbean Ocean. As you talk about each of these men, locate the site of their explorations on the map. Show also where they came from. Amerigo Vespucci was the first to refer to the Americas as new continents.

The questions on page 3 will give the class a chance to review pages 1 and 2. Read the directions together. Correct the activity as soon as the children are finished. The question at the bottom of the page can be discussed as the children color the picture.

ACTIVITIES:

1. Read books on Columbus and discuss them with the class.

2. Have the children reread page 2 and find *three* 3-syllable words. Have them circle the words. Review all vocabulary words and their meanings. Use word cards or the word chart.

Pages 4 and 5: Columbus

CONCEPT: Christopher Columbus discovers a new world.

OBJECTIVE: I can tell how my country began.

TEACHER GOALS: To teach the children
To understand the history of their country, and
To tell who Christopher Columbus was and what he did.

READING INTEGRATION: main idea, noting and recalling details, following directions, listening

VOCABULARY: Americans, brave, Nina, Pinta, Santa Maria, Columbus, sailors

MATERIALS NEEDED: pictures of Columbus and his ships, pencils, construction paper, glue, scissors, crayons, writing tablet

TEACHING PAGES 4 and 5:

Introduce the vocabulary words before reading the page.

Have the children read the paragraphs silently. Check comprehension and vocabulary with the following activity: Each child should have a red, blue, green, and orange crayon. Give these oral directions.

1. Put a blue line under an action word that tells how Columbus came to America. (sailed)

2. Put a green box around the word that tells what the Nina, the Pinta, and the Santa Maria were. (ships)

3. Put a red circle around the word that tells the name of the new land that Columbus discovered. (America)

4. Put an orange 4 behind the word that tells what people are called who live in America. (Americans)

CHRISTOPHER COLUMBUS

Christopher Columbus lived long ago.
He was a very brave man.
He sailed across the ocean
with three small ships.
His ships were called the Nina,
the Pinta, and the Santa Maria.

page 4 (four)

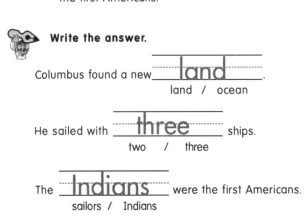

Columbus found a new land.
He had discovered America.
He met the people who lived
in the new land.
Columbus called them Indians.
The Indians were
the first Americans.

Write the answer.

Columbus found a new ___land___.
                                land / ocean

He sailed with ___three___ ships.
                         two / three

The ___Indians___ were the first Americans.
           sailors / Indians

page 5 (five)

107

Have the children complete the activity on page 5. Check both the listening and the written activity as soon as all the children are finished.

ACTIVITIES:

1. *Art Project:* Review what has been learned about Columbus. Have the children draw or paint an ocean background on 12" x 18" paper. Using construction paper, have them cut out the three ships Columbus brought to America. The ships should be small enough to fit on the background. Cut three slits in the "ocean" and partially insert each ship in a slit. Glue the ship to the background or attach them with paper fasteners. The second method allows the children to make the ships rock back and forth.

2. Have the children write a story about Christopher Columbus in their writing tablets. Tell why he is an important person in America's history.

3. Read more about Columbus.

Pages 6 and 7: The Pilgrims

CONCEPT: The Pilgrims

OBJECTIVE: I can tell how my country began.

TEACHER GOALS: To teach the children
To tell why the Pilgrims came to the United States,
To tell who the Pilgrims were,
To understand the reasons why the Pilgrims were thankful, and
To appreciate the relationship between the Indians and the Pilgrims.

READING INTEGRATION: main idea, noting and recalling details, syllables, speaking in a group

VOCABULARY: free, Mayflower, Pilgrims, Plymouth, Squanto (corn, worship)

MATERIALS NEEDED: crayons, pictures and bulletin board cut out prints of Pilgrims and Indians, books about the Pilgrims, milk cartons (1/2 pint size), scissors, glue, construction paper, drawing paper, writing tablet

TEACHING PAGES 6 and 7:
The story of the Pilgrims is one that is fairly familiar to the children. As they read pages 6 and 7, they should be given the chance to talk about things they remember about the Pilgrims. Read the two pages together. Question the class about where the Pilgrims came from and why they came to America. Use the world map to point out the countries of England and Holland. Show the route the Pilgrims sailed in coming to the new world. Stress to the children that Christians today should be thankful for the courage and faith of the Pilgrims who lived so long ago. They were willing to give up everything, even their lives, for freedom to worship their God.

The picture of page 7 shows Squanto, who became an especially good friend to

THE PILGRIMS

More people came
to the new land.
They were called Pilgrims.
The Pilgrims loved God.
In their own country
they could not worship God
in their own way.
They wanted to be free
to worship God.

One hundred (100) Pilgrims came
to America in a very small ship.
The ship was called the Mayflower.
The Pilgrims named
their town Plymouth.

page 6 (six)

The Pilgrim's friend, Squanto, showed them how to plant corn and other food.

Color the picture.

Talk about other ways the Indians helped the Pilgrims.

page 7 (seven)

109

the Pilgrims. Without his help, they may all have died. He spoke English and understood the ways of white men. The story of how this came to be is one that the children will enjoy.

As the children color the picture, discuss the question on the bottom of page 7.

ACTIVITIES:

1. Build a Pilgrim village using milk cartons for the basic house. Construction paper and other scraps can be used for the details. Most books about the Pilgrims give good clear pictures of what their houses and fort looked like.

2. Draw a map of the Plymouth village after it has been built.

3. Find a story about the Pilgrims trip to America or their first year in the United States. Have the children discuss travel then and how people would travel now.

4. Write (in the writing tablets) thank-you prayers to God for His many blessings today.

5. Read books about Squanto and Indian life at the time of the Pilgrims' arrival in America.

Pages 8 and 9: Activity Pages

VOCABULARY: Thanksgiving, thankful

MATERIALS NEEDED: vocabulary cards, pocket chart, 9-inch paper plates, pencils, construction paper, writing tablets, three paper fasteners for each child, scissors, Worksheet 1

TEACHING PAGES 8 and 9:

Before coloring page 8 and discussing the question, it might be helpful to read a story to the children about the Pilgrims' first year in their new home. Emphasize especially the hardships they were willing to suffer in order to be free. It is often difficult for children and even adults to begin to realize what it would be like without the many freedoms we often take for granted. Emphasize the friendship between the Pilgrims and the Indians. In spite of very different ways of life, they were able to help each other. The children might enjoy learning more about the way of life of the Indians who lived near the Pilgrims from books in the library. The *Highlights Handbook About American Indians* is one source for this information.

As the children color the picture on page 8, discuss the question at the bottom. List their answers on the board. Were the Pilgrims thankful for the same things the children are thankful for?

Read the directions on page 9 together. After the children have completed the page, check and correct it.

ACTIVITIES:

1. Have the children divide their writing paper into three columns. Write *1, 2,* or *3* at the top of each column. Post the vocabulary cards in the pocket chart where everyone can see them. The words should be written in the columns according to the numbers of syllables in each word (*Example*: Squanto would be in column 2).

Follow the dots. Color the picture.

What were the pilgrims thankful for?

page 8 (eight)

Write 1, 2, 3 to show who came first, second, and third.

Match the pictures.

page 9 (nine)

2. Divide a pocket chart into three columns. Number each column 1, 2, or 3. Review the concept of syllables. Have the children place the vocabulary cards into the right column according to the number of syllables in each word. This activity can be a small group activity or a whole class activity.

3. *Art Project:* Make thankfulness turkeys. The turkey body is 9-inch plate. The body may be colored any color. Each child should then cut a head and feet (Worksheet 1) from red or orange construction paper. A pattern for the head and feet is included with the Worksheets or the children can design their own. After cutting out the head and feet, they are attached with paper fasteners or glue. Each child then makes a tail full of feathers. The individual feathers may be cut from a variety of colors of construction paper. On each feather the children should print the names of things for which they are thankful. The feathers are then glued to the turkey body. These colorful turkeys can be a daily reminder of how much each child has to be thankful for.

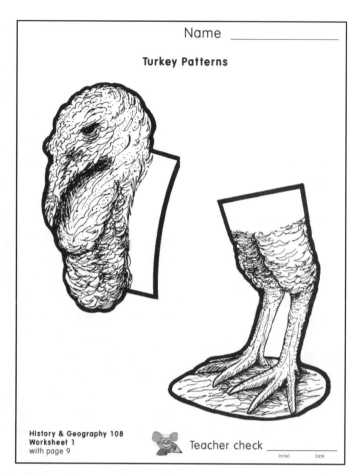

Name _____

Turkey Patterns

History & Geography 108
Worksheet 1
with page 9

Teacher check _____
Initial   Date

Pages 10 and 11: Mayflower Compact

CONCEPT: laws in the new world

OBJECTIVE: I can tell why people need rules.

TEACHER GOALS: To teach the children
To tell about the Mayflower Compact,
To understand why everyone needs rules, and
To understand what a city with no rules or laws would be like.

BIBLE REFERENCE: Deuteronomy 6:6

READING INTEGRATION: main idea, noting and recalling details, alphabetical order, speaking in a group, listening

VOCABULARY: Commandments, Compact, list

MATERIALS NEEDED: black construction paper, white crepe paper, colored construction paper, scissors, glue, large grocery sacks, Worksheet 2, pencils

TEACHING PAGES 10 and 11:

Ask the children to tell what laws are. Talk about why people *NEED* laws (man's sinful nature). Discuss what would happen if a place had no laws.

Remind the class that God gave the first set of written laws. Ask the children what God's laws are called. Even if these laws were not written down, God tells us in the Bible that He put His laws in men's hearts (Deuteronomy 6:6).

The Pilgrims, too, needed laws for their new town. Have the children turn to page 10 and read about the Mayflower Compact. If time allows, read a story about the Mayflower to the students.

As the children listen to the story, they can finish the picture of the Mayflower on page 11.

THE MAYFLOWER COMPACT

God gives laws.
His laws tell people how to live.
The Pilgrims needed laws
for their new town.
They asked God's help.
Their laws followed
the Ten Commandments.
Their list of laws was called
the Mayflower Compact.

page 10 (ten)

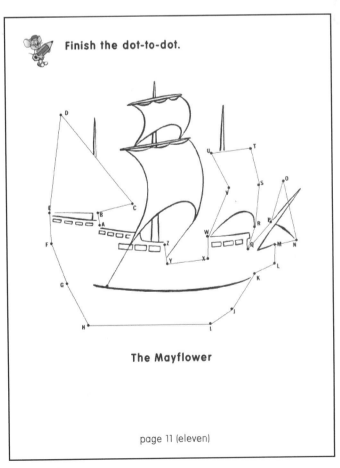

Finish the dot-to-dot.

The Mayflower

page 11 (eleven)

ACTIVITIES:

1.   *Art Project:* Make hats, collars, capes and Indian headbands and shirts. With these simple costumes the children will be ready to reenact the first year of the Pilgrims in their new home.

Pilgrim men's hats can be made of black construction paper. The women's hats can be made of white crepe paper. Cut a circle of white crepe paper with a 12-inch diameter. Using yarn and a needle, put a drawstring around the edge. Carefully pull it to fit the child's head and tie off the yarn in a bow. Indian shirts can be easily made by cutting neck and arm holes in brown grocery sacks.

These sacks are then decorated in Indian designs. Headbands and feathers are made with the construction paper.

2.   Reenact some of the scenes of the Pilgrim's lives during the first year they lived in the United States. Some of these scenes might be used: the first meeting with Samoset and other Indians; Squanto teaching the Pilgrims how to fish, make nets, plant corn, and so on; Pilgrims and Indians hunting; the first Thanksgiving feast.

3.   Read books on the Pilgrims and discuss them with the class.

4.   Together write a play about the Pilgrims' first-year experiences in the new world. Perform the play for parents and other classes.

5.   Provide Worksheet 2 as a vocabulary review. Let the children do the page independently. Check together, discuss the pictures, and drill words that prove difficult.

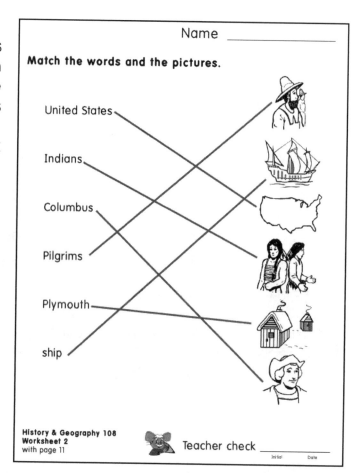

Name _____

Match the words and the pictures.

United States

Indians

Columbus

Pilgrims

Plymouth

ship

History & Geography 108
Worksheet 2
with page 11

Teacher check _____
Initial   Date

Page 12: Self Test 1

CONCEPT: discovery of America

OBJECTIVES:
I can tell how my country began.
I can tell why people need rules.

TEACHER GOAL: To evaluate the children's progress and recall of Part I.

READING INTEGRATION: recalling details, following written directions, sequence, speaking in a group, listening

VOCABULARY: Review all the vocabulary.

MATERIALS NEEDED: pencil flannelboard, interfacing material for making flannel-board characters, writing tablet, pocket chart, vocabulary cards for section one.

TEACHING PAGE 12 :
Have the children open their LIFEPACs to page 12. Read the directions together. Identify all illustrations. As the children work on the page, be available to help any child who may have trouble reading the sentences.

Correct the page as soon as the children are finished. Review any areas that may have caused some children problems.

ACTIVITIES:
1. Tell the story of the Pilgrims and the First Thanksgiving using the flannelboard figures. These may be free-hand drawn or traced. After the teacher tells the story one time, the children will enjoy using the figures to tell the story themselves.
2. Write the following groups of words on the board.

a. Columbus
   Pinta
   America

b. Mayflower
   Pilgrims
   laws

c. Indians
   Compact
   brave

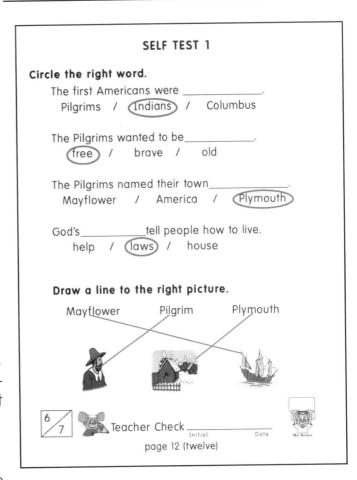

Put the following word cards in the pocket chart: *free, discover, ship.* Review alphabetical order and have the children help to rearrange the word cards into alphabetical order. Then have the children write the three groups of words that are on the board in alphabetical order in their writing tablets.

PART II: HOW THE UNITED STATES BEGAN

Page 13

CONCEPT: how the United States began

OBJECTIVES:
    I can tell the name of my country.
    I can tell how my country began.

TEACHER GOAL: To teach the children a sense of patriotism through their gaining some understanding of the early struggles of our country.

READING INTEGRATION: main idea, noting and recalling details, speaking in a group

VOCABULARY: freedom, war

MATERIALS NEEDED: books and pictures of people and ways of living in colonial times

TEACHING PAGE 13 :

As more and more Europeans came across the ocean, their freedom to make their own laws was slowly taken away from them. The king of England made their laws and sent governors and soldiers to enforce the laws. Finally, about 150 years after the first groups of people came to the United States to live, they voted to become independent. A long, hard war was fought to gain the freedoms we enjoy today.

After introducing page 13, have the children open the LIFEPACs and read page 13 to themselves. Then *ask these questions*:

"Why were the United States people unhappy a long time ago? "

"What did they fight for?"

"What did they call their new country? "

ACTIVITY:

Make a bulletin board display of the pictures of colonial living. Make the books available to the children. Encourage them to find out what life was like in eighteenth-century America.

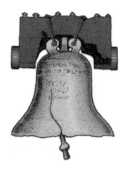

II. HOW THE UNITED STATES BEGAN

Long ago, the people in America
were not free.
The people could not make
their own laws.
People were unhappy.

The Americans fought
for their freedom.
When the war was over,
the new country was free.
The new country was
the United States.
Now the people could make
their own laws.

page 13 (thirteen)

Pages 14 and 15: Activity Pages

VOCABULARY: Independence

MATERIALS NEEDED: crayons, magazines, 9" x 12" drawing paper, pictures of colonial Philadelphia (include Independence Hall) and Boston, glue, scissors

TEACHING PAGES 14 and 15:

Show the children the pictures of colonial America. Talk about each one. Tell what it is. Discuss how the buildings and people are different from those seen today in America.

Have the children open their LIFEPACs to page 14. Talk about the building in the picture. Some of the children may remember what it is. Discuss what happened in Independence Hall in 1776 and why. As the children color, talk about symbols and their meanings, especially symbols of the United States. Review the meaning of the word 'symbol' as it was presented in Social Studies 102. Have the children name other symbols and tell what they stand for.

On page 15, have the children find all the symbols of our country and circle them. When everyone is finished, discuss each symbol as you check the page. A few of the symbols, such as the Canadian flag, may have to be explained to the class.

ACTIVITY:

Art Project: Make a collage of pictures that remind the children of the United States. Pass out the paper and the magazines. Each child should find as many pictures as they can of places or things or people that represent or remind them of the United States. Suggest such things as fireworks, Indians, turkeys, eagles, mountains, the Statue of Liberty, or the flag. Have the children glue the pictures on the Liberty Bell or Washington Monument spaces are covered. When the glue is fairly dry, trace a simple shape of a symbol of liberty on the

Color the picture.

Independence Hall

page 14 (fourteen)

Circle all of the symbols of your country.

Tell what each symbol means.

page 15 (fifteen)

back of the collage. Simple shapes such as the Liberty Bell or Washington Monument work the best. Cut out the shape. Use the finished collages on a bulletin board display entitled *Symbols of Freedom.*

Pages 16 and 17: The First President

CONCEPT: the first President

OBJECTIVE: I can name our first President.

TEACHER GOAL: To teach the children to tell about George Washington.

READING INTEGRATION: main idea, noting and recalling details, speaking in a group, listening

VOCABULARY: George Washington, leader, President, wise

MATERIALS NEEDED: pictures and books about Washington and other well-known men and women of colonial United States, pictures of colonial living, crayons, Worksheet 3

TEACHING PAGES 16 and 17:

Have the children open their books to pages 16 and 17. Ask them who they see in the picture on page 16. Ask them if they can point to the same man in the picture on page 17. Show other pictures of Washington at different ages, if possible.

Discuss the picture on page 17. Explain that the men are signing a paper called the Constitution. Talk about the Constitution, what it is, and why it is important. Mention the Bill of Rights and its importance to all United States citizens, then and today. Ask if the children recognize any other people in the picture. Some may recognize Benjamin Franklin.

Read page 16 together. Discuss the page. At this point you may want to read a book about George Washington to give the children a little more insight into what kind of person he was.

Give the children time to color page 17.

THE FIRST PRESIDENT

The people of the United States
needed a leader.
They chose George Washington.
He was the first President.

President Washington was
a wise leader.
He helped make the laws.
He helped make the country strong,

Today, George Washington is called
"The Father of His Country."

page 16 (sixteen)

 Color this picture.

Talk about what is happening in the picture.

page 17 (seventeen)

ACTIVITIES:

1. Pass out Worksheet 3.

As you discuss what it was like to go to school in George Washington's time, the children's appreciation and thankfulness for their own school should increase greatly.

2. Have the children make a hornbook. Use heavy cardboard for the basic paddle. Cut a piece of unlined paper to fit within the top of the paddle shape. Write the alphabet, math problems, memory work, or other daily work on the paper. Glue the paper to the hornbook. Staple a piece of plastic over the top of the paddle. The word hornbook was used because, instead of plastic, a clear sheet of horn was used to cover the paddle.

3. Introduce the children to other famous people of the colonial era through pictures and books. Some figures to include might be Benjamin Franklin, Paul Revere, Betsy Ross, and Thomas Jefferson.

4. Bake some johnnycake. This corn bread was a staple in the diet of Washington's army as well as in the homes of colonial United States.

1 cup cornmeal	1 cup of milk
1/2 cup sugar	1 egg, well beaten
pinch of salt	1/2 teaspoon baking soda
1 teaspoon cream of tartar	1 Tablespoon molasses
1 tablespoon melted butter	

Sift dry ingredients together in a bowl. Add the other ingredients and beat well. Pour into a shallow greased baking pan and bake in a hot oven (375°F.) for 30 minutes.

Name _____

Going to school in colonial days.

The children read their lessons from boards called **hornbooks.**

History & Geography 108
Worksheet 3
with page 17

Teacher check _____

Initial   Date

Pages 18 and 19: Abraham Lincoln

CONCEPT: Abraham Lincoln

OBJECTIVE I can tell why people need rules.

TEACHER GOAL: To teach the children to appreciate the struggle of our nation to finally fulfill the Declaration of Independence for all people.

READING INTEGRATION: main idea, noting and recalling details, following written directions

VOCABULARY: Abraham Lincoln

MATERIALS NEEDED: pencils, crayons, pictures of Lincoln and the Lincoln Memorial, a penny, Worksheet 4

TEACHING PAGES 18 and 19:

Hold up the picture of the Lincoln Memorial. Ask if any children know who the statue represents. Discuss why such a big statue and building was built in memory of this man. Explain a little about the Civil War and why it was fought. God created all people. Our laws today ensure that all people are free.

Read page 18 together. Help the children to understand that although all our Presidents have not been Christians, God has used them to make our country strong and free. Christians, young and old, should pray for our leaders that God will continue to work through them for the good of the United States and all people in the world.

Page 19 is a review of several historical figures. Read the directions. Then have the children do the page.

ACTIVITIES:

1. We know quite a bit about the childhood of Lincoln, especially concerning his great thirst for knowledge. Pass out Worksheet 4. Talk about the pictures and

ABRAHAM LINCOLN

Abraham Lincoln lived over 100 years ago.
He was a very wise President.
He knew that the laws of our country
must work for all people.
He helped to make all people free.
He helped to make our country strong.

page 18 (eighteen)

 Circle the right picture.

He is called "The Father of His Country."

He helped to make all people free.

He discovered America.

page 19 (nineteen)

read the sentences. Read other stories and books about Lincoln.

2.   Make a collage mural for the bulletin board about Abraham Lincoln. Include childhood incidents as well as stories about him when he was President. The log cabin of his youth might be made from brown corrugated cardboard. Trees and bushes can be real twigs with green construction paper or crushed green tissue paper for leaves. Cut paper people may be dressed with fabric. The children's imaginations are the only limitation to this project.

Name _____

Abe Lincoln loved to read and learn.
He borrowed books from anyone who would loan him one.

Abe Lincoln was honest and a hard worker. Once a book he borrowed was ruined in the rain. He worked 3 days to pay for the book.

History & Geography 108
Worksheet 4
with page 19

Teacher check _____

Initial   Date

Pages 20 and 21: Laws

CONCEPT: the need for laws

OBJECTIVE: I can tell why People need rules.

TEACHER GOAL: To teach the children to understand the need for rules, both for a country and for their own classrooms.

READING INTEGRATION: main idea, noting and recalling details, following written directions, speaking in a group, listening

VOCABULARY: travel (protect)

MATERIALS NEEDED: vocabulary cards, pocket chart, crayons, pencils

TEACHING PAGES 20 and 21:

Washington, Lincoln and other early leaders of our country realized the importance of laws that guarantee certain basic freedoms to all United States citizens. The Declaration of Independence, the Constitution, and the Bill of Rights all are based on the laws that God laid down for His people in the Bible and wrote in the hearts of people. Without these laws the world would be a frightening place in which to live.

As the children read page 20 together, discuss the consequences of not having any laws or rules. Suggest situations that might arise at school if no laws governed stealing or lying, for instance. Because of sin, God in His love did give us rules. They are for our protection and happiness.

If an encyclopedia is available, look up the Bill of Rights and list on the board all the freedoms it guarantees to United States citizens. Discuss how each one affects the children's lives.

Read the directions on page 21. After the children have finished the first activity, check it.

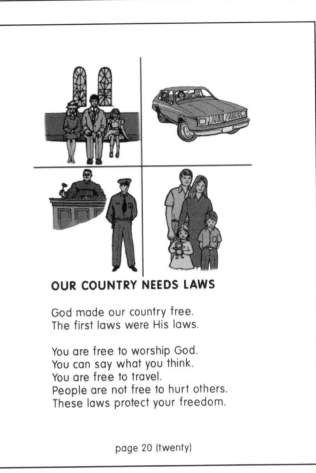

OUR COUNTRY NEEDS LAWS

God made our country free.
The first laws were His laws.

You are free to worship God.
You can say what you think.
You are free to travel.
People are not free to hurt others.
These laws protect your freedom.

page 20 (twenty)

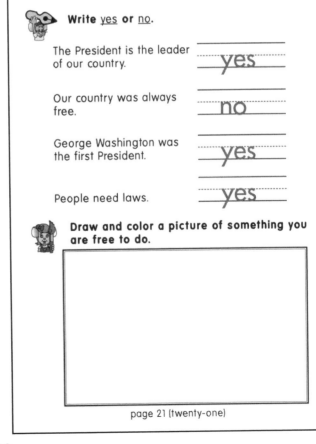

Write <u>yes</u> **or** <u>no</u>.

The President is the leader of our country.   *yes*

Our country was always free.   *no*

George Washington was the first President.   *yes*

People need laws.   *yes*

Draw and color a picture of something you are free to do.

page 21 (twenty-one)

Review sections one and two of the LIFEPAC. Use the objectives listed on page 1 as a guide to questions to (*ask the children*).

"Who can tell the name of the country in which we live?"

"Will someone point to the United States on the map?"

"Who came to America and thought he had found India?"

"Which people came to the United States for freedom of religion?"

"Who was the first President of the United States?"

"Why do people need laws?"

ACTIVITIES:

1. Have the children tell about their pictures on page 21. This may be done in small groups or as a whole class activity.

2. Review the vocabulary words. Write the words on the board or post them in the pocket chart. Give sentence definitions and ask the class to tell which word you are talking about. Have one student come forward and point to the correct word.

Page 22: Self Test 2

CONCEPT: how the United States began

OBJECTIVE:
> I can tell how my country began.
> I can name our first President.
> I can tell why people need rules.

TEACHER GOAL: To evaluate what the children have learned about the early history of their country.

READING INTEGRATION: recalling details, following written directions, sequence

VOCABULARY: Review all the vocabulary words.

MATERIALS NEEDED: pencils, lunch-size paper sacks, crayons, construction paper, glue, scissors, scrap art materials (yarn, cotton balls, fabric, and so on.)

TEACHING PAGE 22:
Have the children turn to page 22 in their LIFEPACs. Read the directions together. Answer any questions about what to do. Identify all illustrations. Allow the children sufficient time to complete the page. Check the page as soon as possible after all are finished.

ACTIVITY:
Make paper bag puppets. Tell each child to think about the different people they have learned about in this LIFEPAC. List some of them on the board. Tell the children that they are going to make paper bag puppets, (see illustration). They should choose one character they have learned about to personify in a puppet. The faces are cut from construction paper with the features either glued on or drawn on with crayon. The face is then glued to the bottom of the bag. Hair can be made of yarn, cotton, or other suitable material. Hats, clothing, arms, legs, and beards may be added. As the children work, give helpful suggestions. For the most part encourage them to use their own imaginations.

PART III: HOW TO SHOW RESPECT FOR YOUR COUNTRY

Pages 23 and 24:

CONCEPT: showing respect for our country

TEACHER GOAL: To teach the children to tell ways of showing respect for their country.

READING INTEGRATION: main idea, noting and recalling detail, following written directions, writing sentences

VOCABULARY: respect, pledge, allegiance

MATERIALS NEEDED: writing tablet, pencils

TEACHING PAGES 23 and 24:

Introduce the vocabulary words by writing them on the board. Discuss the meaning of each one. Although the children may say the Pledge of Allegiance every day, they may not know what it means to pledge allegiance to something. Look the words pledge and allegiance up in a dictionary. Read the definitions and talk about them.

Have the children open their LIFEPACs to page 23. Talk about what the children in the picture are doing. Ask if they have ever seen people salute the flag in a different way than the one in the picture.

Read the page together. Ask the children to repeat back to you the three ways they can show respect for the United States.

The United States is, of course, not the only thing children must learn to respect. Most important of all, they learn ways to show their love and respect for God. Tell the children that when they ask Jesus to come into their hearts and be the ruler of their lives, they are pledging their allegiance to Him. This pledge is one way they show their love and respect for Jesus.

III. HOW TO SHOW RESPECT FOR YOUR COUNTRY

Do you salute the flag?
Can you say the Pledge of Allegiance?
People stand when they sing
our country's song.
Show your love for the United States
by doing these three things.

page 23 (twenty-three)

Give the class time to work on the drawing on page 24. They may want to draw only a few class members. Remind them to put the flag into their picture.

Be sure each child can say the pledge by himself.

ACTIVITIES:

1. In their writing tablets have the children write the three things they can do to show love and respect for their country. They should use complete sentences.

2. Sing patriotic songs.

Draw your class saying the Pledge of Allegiance.

The Pledge of Allegiance

I pledge allegiance to the flag
of the United States of America
and to the republic for which it stands,
one nation under God, indivisible,
with liberty and justice for all.

page 24 (twenty-four)

Page 25: Christian Flag

CONCEPT: the Christian flag

TEACHER GOALS: To teach the children the meaning of the Christian flag and the pledge to the Savior, and to have them memorize the pledge to the Christian flag.

READING INTEGRATION: main idea, listening, speaking in a group

VOCABULARY: (Christian, Kingdom, crucified, risen, liberty)

MATERIALS NEEDED: crayons religious symbols patterns, construction paper, glue, scissors,

TEACHING PAGE 25:

Have the children turn to page 25 in their LIFEPACs. Ask if any of them have ever seen a flag like the one on page 25. Have them tell where they saw one.

Many churches display the Christian flag along with the United States flag. This flag is one way of saying "we as Christians give honor, first to God, and secondly, to the country God has given us." (*Talk about the colors of the flag as the children color it.*)

"What does the white stand for?" (purity and holiness of God)

"What does the blue stand for?" (heaven)

"What does the red cross symbolize?" (Jesus' blood shed for our sins on the cross at Calvary)

Read the pledge together. Talk about what it means. In effect it is really a pledge to our Savior, Jesus Christ. Have the students memorize the pledge. Use it as part of your daily opening activities.

ACTIVITIES:

1. *Art Project:* Make a Christian banner or flag. Each child can design their own flag or banner that will remind people of Jesus

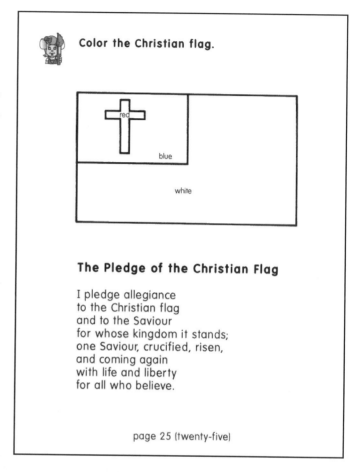

Color the Christian flag.

red

blue

white

The Pledge of the Christian Flag

I pledge allegiance
to the Christian flag
and to the Saviour
for whose kingdom it stands;
one Saviour, crucified, risen,
and coming again
with life and liberty
for all who believe.

page 25 (twenty-five)

their Savior. Stencils may be used or the children may want to design their own symbols. The shape of the banner or flag should also be left up to the child. Several shapes may be suggested for them to choose from. The illustration shows some possible shapes. The flags and banners may be displayed around the school and classroom before they are taken home.

2. The Pledge to the Bible is another good pledge for Christians to make daily.

I pledge allegiance to the Bible God's Holy Word. I make it a lamp unto my feet and a light unto my path. I will hide its word in my heart that I might not sin against God.

Pages 26 and 27: The Flag

CONCEPT: the flag

OBJECTIVE: I can say the Pledge of Allegiance.

TEACHER GOAL: To teach the children to understand the symbolism of the flag

READING INTEGRATION: main idea, noting and recalling detail, following written directions, plurals

VOCABULARY: fifty, stand, straight, stripes, thirteen (heart)

MATERIALS NEEDED: crayons, pencils, pictures of some of the flags used by the United States colonies before the Revolution, writing tablet

TEACHING PAGES 26 and 27:

Have the children open their LIFEPACs to pages 26 and 27. Read the first paragraph together. *Ask these questions*:

"What do you see on the top of page 26?"

"How many stripes are on the flag?"

"What color should the stripes be?"

"Who knows how many stars are on the flag?"

"Can anyone tell what each color stands for?" (red for courage, white for liberty, and blue for the heavens or sky)

"Why are there thirteen stripes?"

"Why are there fifty stars?"

Finish reading page 26 and the top of page 27. Ask the children to answer the question and ask why two flags are different. Show the pictures of some of the flags used by the different colonies before we became a nation.

When the children color the flag on page 27, remind them to start with a red stripe.

THE FLAG

This flag is the United States flag.
It is red, white, and blue.
The flag has thirteen stripes
and fifty stars.

Stand up straight when you say
the Pledge of Allegiance.
Put your right hand over your heart.

page 26 (twenty-six)

This picture shows our first flag.
How is it different from
our flag today.

 Color this flag.

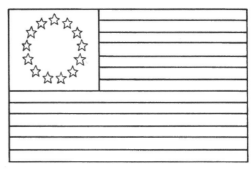

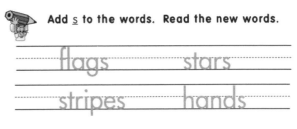 **Add s to the words. Read the new words.**

flags   stars

stripes   hands

page 27 (twenty-seven)

Read the words at the bottom of page 27. Have the children add *s* and read the words one more time together. Discuss how the meanings of the words changed when an *s* was added .

ACTIVITIES:

1. Have the children write sentences in their writing tablets using the plural words on the bottom of page 27.

2. Read a book about the flag. Talk about other holidays that honor the United States flag.

3. The children may enjoy reading or putting on a play about the flag.

Pages 28 and 29: Songs

CONCEPT: songs about America

TEACHER GOALS: To teach the children
To name the national anthem, and
To sing several songs about the United States.

READING INTEGRATION: main idea, noting and recalling details, following written directions

VOCABULARY: Francis Scott Key, Star-Spangled Banner

MATERIALS NEEDED: pencils, banner paper, crayons, box screen, writing tablet, Worksheet 5

TEACHING PAGES 28 and 29:

Have the children open their LIFEPACs to page 28. Use the picture as a basis for telling the story of how our national anthem was written. Read the page together and talk about it. Have the children list ways they can show their love for the country they live in.

Many songs have been written in honor of the United States. In some, such as the national anthem, we sing about symbols (the flag). Others, such as "America," speak of the beauty and diversity of nature in the United States.

ACTIVITIES:

1. Learn and sing the "Star-Spangled Banner".

2. Write prayers in the writing tablet showing thankfulness for our free and beautiful nation.

3. Pass out Worksheet 5. Read the directions together. After the children have completed and checked this page, review all the vocabulary words in this LIFEPAC.

SONGS ABOUT OUR COUNTRY

Our country has a special song.
It is called the "Star Spangled Banner."
Francis Scott Key wrote the words.
He loved the United States.
He was happy to be an American.

page 28 (twenty-eight)

Do you know this song?
Sing it with your class.

O say can you see,
By the dawn's early light,
What so proudly we hailed,
At the twilight's last gleaming,
Whose broad stripes and bright stars,
Through the perilous fight,
O'er the ramparts we watched,
Were so gallantly streaming?
And the rockets' red glare,
The bombs bursting in air,

Gave proof through the night,
That our flag was still there.
O say, does that star-spangled banner Yet wave,
O'er the land of the free,
And the home of the brave?

 Draw a picture from this song.

page 29 (twenty-nine)

Name _____

Find the right word and write it on the line.

flag	Pilgrim	president
Indian	pledge	United States

Pilgrim   president

flag   pledge

Indian   United States

History & Geography 108
Worksheet 5
with page 29

Teacher check _____
Initial   Date

Pages 30 and 31: Holidays

CONCEPT: national holidays

TEACHER GOAL: To teach the children to name several national holidays.

READING INTEGRATION: main idea, noting and recalling details, following written directions, sequence

VOCABULARY: Independence Day, holidays, (July, birthday)

MATERIALS NEEDED: Worksheet 6, apples, lemon juice, sugar, cinnamon, hot plate, large kettle, water, spoon, measuring spoons, record or book: *The Story of Johnny Appleseed,* crayons, writing tablets

TEACHING PAGES 30 and 31:

Our country has many national holidays that people celebrate every year. List as many as the children and teacher can remember. Check a calendar for a complete list. Distinguish between national holidays and Christian holidays.

Read page 30 in the LIFEPAC. Here only two holidays are mentioned. Talk about the ways people observe these holidays. How do Christians observe Thanksgiving that is different from the way non-Christians observe the day?

Besides national holidays, the calendar lists many days set aside to remember people who have had a special part in the history of our country. One of these special people is John Chapman, otherwise known as Johnny Appleseed. A great deal of legend is mixed with fact in the story of John Chapman but it's a story the children will enjoy. Learning a little about this United States pioneer will be an enjoyable conclusion to this LIFEPAC about our nation's early history and its people .

HOLIDAYS

One special holiday
is Independence Day.
It comes on July 4th.
It is the birthday
of the United States.

Another special holiday is
Thanksgiving.
It is a day to say
"thank you" to God.

page 30 (thirty)

Find these things in the picture.

flag   liberty bell   Mayflower   eagle

turkey   George Washington   Abraham Lincoln   Indian

page 31 (thirty-one)

Review symbols of the country. Have the children turn to page 31. Read the directions and names of the symbols. This page does not have to be checked.

ACTIVITIES:

1. Listen to the record or read about Johnny Appleseed.

2. Make applesauce as a classroom project. Peel and slice 2 quarts of apple pieces. Put 2 cups of water and the apples in a large kettle. Add 1 cup of sugar, a pinch of salt, 2 teaspoons of lemon juice. and 1/4 teaspoon of cinnamon.

Cook all the ingredients until the apples are tender. Mash the apples with a potato masher or an electric mixer. Serve warm and enjoy.

3. Pass out Worksheet 6. Discuss the pictures in order. Have the children draw what they think will happen next to the apple trees. Then the children should write about the picture they drew in their writing tablets.

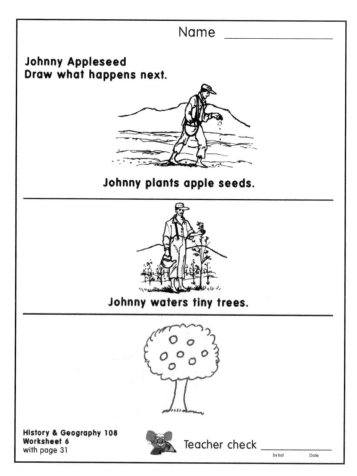

Name _____

**Johnny Appleseed
Draw what happens next.**

Johnny plants apple seeds.

Johnny waters tiny trees.

**History & Geography 108
Worksheet 6**
with page 31

Teacher check _____
Initial   Date

Page 32: Self Test 3

CONCEPT: show respect for your country

OBJECTIVE: I can say the Pledge of Allegiance.

TEACHER GOAL: To evaluate the children's recall of section three and the rest of the LIFEPAC.

READING INTEGRATION: following written directions, recalling details

TEACHING PAGE 32:

Have the children turn to page 32 in their LIFEPACs. Read the directions together. Answer any questions about what to do. Identify all illustrations. Allow the children sufficient time to complete the page. Check the page as soon as possible after all are finished.

Review any concepts that have been missed before administering the LIFEPAC Test.

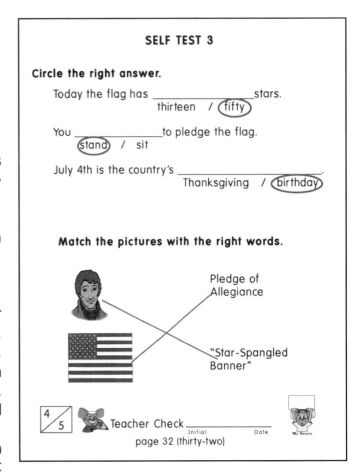

Page 33: Take Home Activity Page

MATERIALS NEEDED: scissors, crayons, tape

TEACHING PAGE 33:

Have the children color the puppets and cut them out. Make sure they do not cut off the tabs.

Help the children fit the puppets around their fingers. Tape the tabs to the right size.

The children may use the puppets to reenact the Pilgrim stories, the story of Squanto, or the First Thanksgiving. They may take them home and act out the stories for their families.

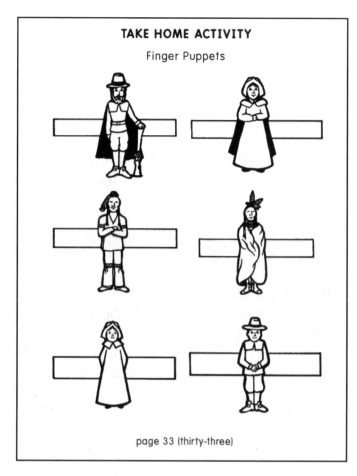

TAKE HOME ACTIVITY

Finger Puppets

page 33 (thirty-three)

LIFEPAC TEST AND ALTERNATE LIFEPAC TEST

Administer the test to the class as a group. Ask to have directions read or read them to the class. In either case, be sure that the children clearly understand. Put examples on the board if it seems necessary. Give ample time for each activity to be completed before going on to the next.

Correct immediately and discuss with the child.

Review any concepts that have been missed.

Give those children who do not achieve the 80% score additional copies of the worksheets and a list of vocabulary words to study. A parent or a classroom helper should help in the review.

When the child is ready, give the Alternate LIFEPAC Test. Use the same procedure as for the LIFEPAC TEST.

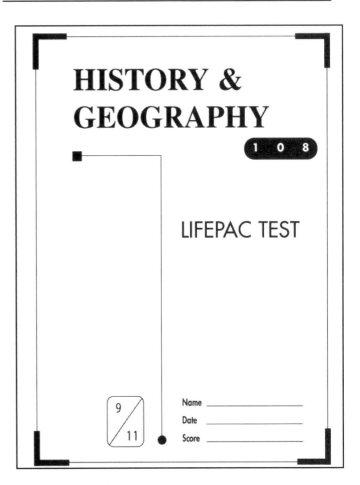

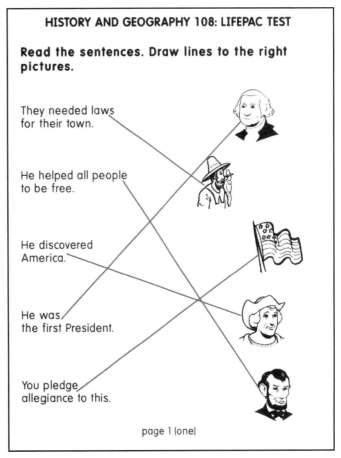

page 1 (one)

137

Circle the right word.

Independence Day is_____ birthday.
Columbus's / (America's)

Laws are made to_____ people.
hurt / (help)

The name of my country is_____.
Plymouth / (United States)

Write 1, 2, 3 to show what happened first, second, and third.

1    3    2

page 2 (two)

NOTES

page 3 (three)

HISTORY & GEOGRAPHY

1 0 8

ALTERNATE LIFEPAC TEST

10 / 13

Name _____

Date _____

Score _____

**HISTORY & GEOGRAPHY 108:
ALTERNATE LIFEPAC TEST**

Write 1, 2, 3 **to show what happened** first, second, **and** third.

_____2_____   _____1_____   _____3_____

Write the right word.

Squanto was the_____ friend.
President's / (Pilgrim's)

Columbus had _____ ships.
one / two / (three)

The Mayflower Compact was a list of _____.
people / (rules)

page 1 (one)

Circle yes **or** no.

Rules and laws protect people.   (yes) / no

The first President was Lincoln.   yes / (no)

You can say the Pledge of
Allegiance   (yes) / no

Match the names an d the pictures.

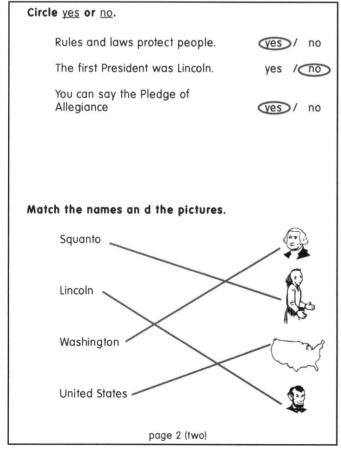

Squanto

Lincoln

Washington

United States

page 2 (two)

NOTES

page 3 (three)

139

Page 1: I Live in the World

CONCEPT: Introduction to I Live in the World

OBJECTIVE: To introduce all of the objectives.

TEACHER GOAL: To teach the children to review the structure and use of a table of contents.

READING INTEGRATION: table of contents, main idea

VOCABULARY: world, Japan, Mexico, globe

MATERIALS NEEDED: pictures of people from many places around the world, globe, world map, writing tablet, pencils

TEACHING PAGE 1:

Have the children turn to the Contents Page in the LIFEPAC, I Live In The World. Read the title together and discuss the word *world.* Show a globe for any who do not know what the word *world* means.

Review the purpose of a contents page. *Ask specific questions about this Table of Contents.*

"What are the three sections of this LIFEPAC?"

"What will you learn about on page 11?"

"What are some things you learn about Mexico?

"What other country are you going to learn about?"

"What page does the part about Japan begin on?"

Have the children turn to page 1. Discuss the pictures of the children at the top. The first girl is from Sweden. She wears the crown of candles as part of the Swedish Christmas celebration. Point out where Sweden is located on a map or globe. The next girl is an Eskimo. Locate the land of the Eskimos on a map. The last child is an Indian boy

---

I LIVE IN THE WORLD

The world is filled with people.

God makes everyone different.

In some ways everyone is alike.

You will read how people are different.

You will read how people are alike.

OBJECTIVES

1. I can tell about a globe.
2. I can tell ways all people are alike.
3. I can tell ways all people may be different.
4. I can tell how people live in Japan and Mexico.

page 1 (one)

---

from South America, Peru or Bolivia. Find his home on the map. Talk about ways all three of these children are alike and ways they are different.

Read page 1 together. Put up the pictures of people of many nations. Mention one or two ways they are all alike and one or two ways they are all different. Ask the children to repeat some of the objectives of this LIFEPAC. This is a good time to remind the children that God sent His Son to save all nations (John 3:16).

ACTIVITIES:

1. Have the children write several sentences in their writing tablets about how they are like the people in the pictures that were posted. They should also write several sentences about how they are different from those people. Allow time for the children to read and compare their sentences in small groups.

2. Post the world map where all the children can have easy access to it. Label the pictures of the people from other nations with the name of their country. Have the children try to locate the different countries on the map or on a globe.

PART I: THE WORLD AROUND US

Pages 2 and 3:

CONCEPT: The world around us

OBJECTIVE: I can tell about a globe.

TEACHER GOALS: To teach the children
To appreciate all God has created for them, and
To recognize the country in which they live.

BIBLE REFERENCE: Genesis, Chapter 1

READING INTEGRATION: main idea, noting and recalling details, written directions, speaking in a group, listening

VOCABULARY: earth

MATERIALS NEEDED: Bible, globe, picture of solar system, assorted colors of construction paper, crayons, world map, flannelboard, magazines, white paper, glue, scissors, pencils

TEACHING PAGES 2 and 3:

Write the word *earth* and *world* on the board. Show the picture of the solar system. Ask the children to tell what they see in the picture. Explain the planets. Each one has a name. You might mention several of them. One of the planets is called Earth. Point to our planet. As part of the heavens and earth, God made it in a special way so we would have all the things we need to live a happy life. Have the children name some of the things we need to live a happy life. Have the children name some of the things they think they need to live a happy life. Write their responses on the board. Read the creation story from Genesis. As you read what was created each day, write it on the board. When you have finished the story, ask

I. THE WORLD AROUND US

Our world is very big.
It is called Earth.
It has land and water.
God made the earth for us.
Let's find out
what the earth looks like!

page 2 (two)

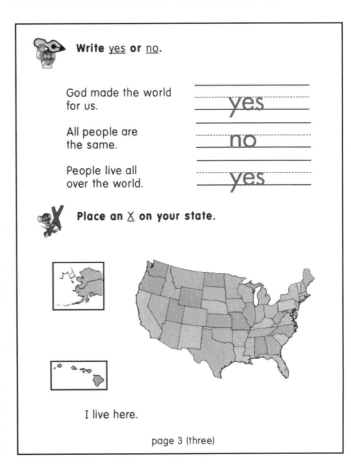

Write <u>yes</u> **or** <u>no</u>.

God made the world for us.   yes

All people are the same.   no

People live all over the world.   yes

Place an <u>X</u> **on your state.**

I live here.

page 3 (three)

the children again what things are needed for people to live a happy life. Compare the Biblical list with the children's list.

Have the children open their LIFEPACs to page 2. Read the page together. Talk about the earth God made for us. Talk about the illustration. Compare the illustration to the globe. Do the exercise on page 3 as a review of what the children have read so far. After they have completed the dot-to-dot, identify the two countries (Canada, United States). Find them on the map and on the globe. Have the children put an *X* on the country in which they live.

ACTIVITIES:

1. Tell the story of creation on a flannelboard. Allow the children to tell the story after you. Give several children a chance to do this. It will help to plant the sequence of events in their minds.

2. *Art Project:* Make a World We Live In collage. Cut pictures out of the magazines of as many different kinds of places as the children can find. Glue these randomly all over a piece of 9" x 12" construction paper. Use them for a bulletin board display entitled God's Beautiful World.

3. Give each child seven white circles about six inches in diameter Have the children review the sequence of creation. Have them draw and color one day of creation on each circle. Staple these together into a booklet. Divide the class into small groups. Give each child a chance to share his booklet with the other children in the group.

Pages 4 and 5: The Globe

CONCEPT: the globe

OBJECTIVE: I can tell about a globe.

TEACHER GOALS: To teach the children
To use a globe for locating countries of the world, and
To understand the significance of the colors blue and green on a globe.

READING INTEGRATION: main idea, noting and recalling details, writing sentences, listening, speaking in a group, following oral and written directions

VOCABULARY: (globe, north, south)

MATERIALS NEEDED: globe, world map, Worksheet 1, crayons, writing tablet, flashcards of the four directions, words, pencils

TEACHING PAGES 4 and 5:

Hold up a globe. Ask the class to tell you what it is. Ask what it represents. Explain that the real world is a very large place. The globe helps us to see what the earth would look like from the moon or another point in space.

Have the children open their LIFEPACs to page 4. Discuss the picture. Read the page together. Discuss it. *Ask the children:*

"Why is a globe round?"

"What does a globe show us?"

"What does the blue on the globe represent?"

"What does the green on the globe represent?"

"What is the name of the world that is shown by this globe?"

Read the directions on the top of page 5 together. Give the children time to answer the questions. Check the answers when all

THE GLOBE

The children are looking at a globe.
A globe is round.
It shows us what the earth
looks like.
It shows where there is land and
where there is water.

page 4 (four)

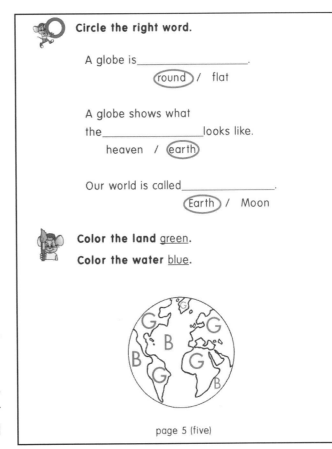

Circle the right word.

A globe is_____.
(round) / flat

A globe shows what
the_____looks like.
heaven / (earth)

Our world is called_____.
(Earth) / Moon

Color the land green.
Color the water blue.

page 5 (five)

145

the children are finished. Read the directions at the bottom of the page and give the children time to complete the activity independently. The teacher should walk around the room as the children are working to give assistance where it is needed. Have the classroom globe in plain sight of the children for reference purposes.

ACTIVITIES:

1. Introduce the children to the directions North and South on the globe. Use the classroom globe and Worksheet 1 for this activity. Pass out the Worksheets. Compare the picture on the Worksheet to the globe. Let the children find each country that they see on their map and point to it on the globe. Ask the children where they think the North Pole is located. Identify it on the globe by marking it with chalk or taping a sign to it. Do the same with the South Pole. Point out that when we look at the globe, the North Pole is at the top and the South Pole is at the bottom. Sometimes the North Pole is called the top of the world. The same thing is true on a flat map like the one the children have in front of them. Tell the children to write the word *NORTH* on the line at the top of the Worksheet and the word *SOUTH* on the line at the bottom. Give the children the following directions for marking on their Worksheet.

a. Put a big green *X* on the United States, the country in which we live.

b. Color the country that is north of the United States *blue*.

c. Color the country that is closest to the North Pole *Yellow*.

d. Color the country that is closest to the South Pole *red*.

e. Color the country that is just south of the United States *orange* .

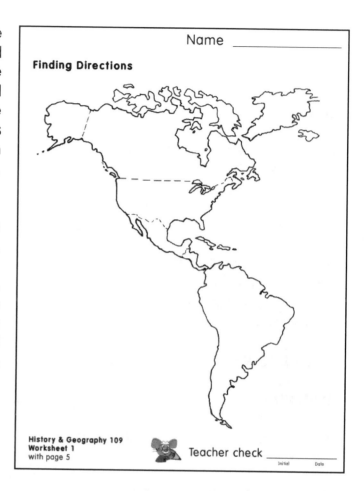

Name _____

Finding Directions

History & Geography 109
Worksheet 1
with page 5   Teacher check _____
                                              Initial   Date

2. Practice direction finding in the classroom. Label the walls of the room North, South, East, and West. First just have the children turn to the various directions as you say them. Later have them locate objects in the room by telling if the object is on the North, South, East, or West side of the room. Play a guessing game using the children a chance to make up the sentences in their writing tablets using the directions. Say, for example, "I'm thinking of something that starts with a *b* and is hanging on the West wall." Give the children a chance to make up the directions for the other students.

3. Have the children write sentences in their writing tablets using the words North, South, East, and West.

Pages 6 and 7: Many Kinds of Places

CONCEPT: many kinds of places

TEACHER GOAL: To teach the children about some of the different places that God has created for people to live.

READING INTEGRATION: main idea, noting and recalling details, following written directions, writing stories, dictionary work, speaking in a group

VOCABULARY: mountains, flat, rainy (dry)

MATERIALS NEEDED: writing tablet, drawing paper, crayons, pictures of different kinds of places (the ocean, deserts, mountains, jungles, forests, plains, frozen tundra, and so on), pencils

TEACHING PAGES 6 and 7:

Display the pictures of the different kinds of places on the earth. Name and talk about each one. *Ask:*

"Is it cold or hot?"

"Is it wet or dry?"

"What kind of plants and animals live there?"

"Do people live there?"

Compare where you live with the different places shown in the pictures. Let the children share personal experiences about various places they have lived or visited. Use the map to point out the areas of the world where it is very cold, or wet, or hot. Encourage the children to look at the books on the book table that have to do with these different places in the world.

Read page 6 together. Talk about the pictures in relationship to what is read and has been discussed. Write the words *hot, dry, mountain,* and *cold* on the board. Have the children read them and use them in oral sentences about the earth.

MANY KINDS OF PLACES

God has made
many kinds of places.
Some places have tall
mountains.
Other places are very flat.

Some places may be very hot
or very cold.
Some places are wet and rainy.
Other places are very dry.

page 6 (six)

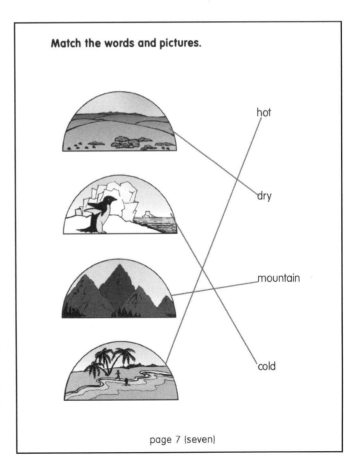

Match the words and pictures.

hot

dry

mountain

cold

page 7 (seven)

Turn to page 7 and read the directions. The children should draw lines from the pictures to the words. Check the page as soon as they are finished.

ACTIVITIES:

1.   Have the children write a story in their writing tablets about one kind of place in the world. It should be a place they have visited or have lived. It might be the area they are living in now. Have them tell about the land, the weather, and the kinds of plants and animals that are found in the place.

2.   Pass out drawing paper and have the children illustrate the story they wrote for activity one. When they are finished, have each child share his picture with the whole class or with a small group.

3.   Make books about the different kinds of places in the world available to the class. Some of these may be read to the class or even assigned as outside reading to more accelerated students. Those students could report back to the class about what they read.

Pages 8 and 9: Many Countries

CONCEPT: many countries in the world

OBJECTIVE: I can tell about a globe.

TEACHER GOALS: To teach the children
   To distinguish different countries on a globe or map, and
   To help them recognize Japan and Mexico.

READING INTEGRATION: main idea, noting and recalling details, written directions, dictionary work

VOCABULARY: smallest, closer (Mexico, Japan)

MATERIALS NEEDED: globe, world map, Worksheet 2, flashcards, word chart, alphabet chart, pencils

TEACHING PAGES 8 and 9:
   Using the globe and the map, talk about how different countries are distinguished by color and boundary lines. Talk about some of the different countries and where they are located. Indicate islands that are countries such as England and Ireland.
   Point to Japan and show that this country is made up of a whole group of islands. Review what the color blue stands for on maps and globes. Tell the children the name of the ocean surrounding Japan. Point out Japan's location in relation to the United States.
   Talk about the neighboring countries to the United States. Identify these neighbors and locate them on the map. Give the children a chance to share any experiences they may have had visiting or living in any of these countries.
   Have the children open their LIFEPACs to page 8 and read the page together. Answer the questions that are raised during

MANY COUNTRIES

The people of the world live
in many countries.
Look at the three countries marked
on the globe.
Which one is the United States?
The other countries are
Mexico and Japan.
Which one is the smallest?
Which one is closer
to the United States?

page 8 (eight)

Write <u>yes</u> or <u>no</u>.

Japan is smaller than
the United States.   yes

Mexico is far away
from the United States.   no

Japan is close
to the United States.   no

Mexico is bigger
than Japan.   yes

page 9 (nine)

the reading. Have the children locate the various countries on the globe in their books and on the classroom map.

Have the children turn to page 9. Before assigning this page to the class, practice using comparative words for different things in the classroom. *(Example:* "Is the window or the blackboard farther away from your desk?") Questions about the map may also be used as a preparation for the page. (*Example*: "Is Canada smaller than the United States?") Have the children work the page independently. Check the page together when everyone is finished. If the children have a great deal of difficulty deciding whether something is larger or smaller, farther away or closer, do some measuring activities using the map and the globe. String stretched between the different countries will show which are closer and which are farther away. Cutout shapes of the countries placed one on top of another will help the children to see which are larger and which are smaller.

ACTIVITY:

Worksheet 2 is a practice page for the part one vocabulary words as well as for dictionary work. Review the vocabulary words from section one using flashcards or a word chart.

Put the following group of words on the board: *earth, globe, flat.* Underline the first letter in each word. Review the concept of alphabetical order. Have the children decide which word of the three on the board comes first alphabetically. Write the word in a second column on the board. Decide which word will come next and write it under the first word. Write the third word.

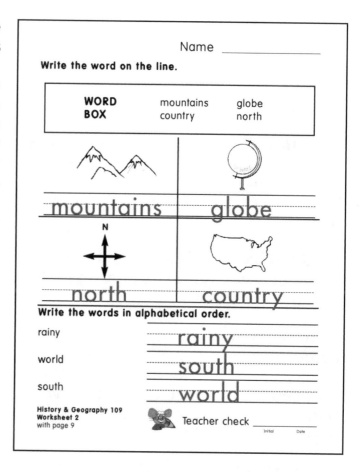

Write three more words on the board: *dry, cold, hot.* Follow the same procedure as with the first three. If necessary, practice with as many more groups of words as the children need to be able to do the activity independently.

Pass out the Worksheet. Give the directions and make sure everyone understands what to do on both parts of the page. Check the Worksheet as soon as everyone is finished.

Page 10: Self Test 1

CONCEPT: the world around us

OBJECTIVE: I can tell about a globe.

TEACHER GOAL: To evaluate the children's understanding of part one of this LIFEPAC.

READING INTEGRATION: recalling detail, following written directions, speaking in a group

VOCABULARY: Review all the new words.

MATERIALS NEEDED: writing tablet, drawing paper, crayons, pencils

TEACHING PAGE 10:

   Have the children turn to page 10 in their LIFEPACs. Read the directions together. Answer any questions about what to do. Identify all illustrations. Allow the children sufficient time to complete the page. Check the page as soon as possible after all are finished.

ACTIVITIES:

   1.   Review any areas of the test that may have caused difficulty. Go back in the LIFEPAC to the pages that cover the trouble-spots. Reread and discuss the subject causing the difficulty.

   2.   Have the children write a story in their writing tablets about what the world looks like where they live. Have them tell about their own neighborhood and about the geographic area in which their school is located.

   3.   Have the children draw pictures to go with their stories. Stories and pictures should be shared with the class or in small groups. The stories and pictures can also be used for a bulletin board display.

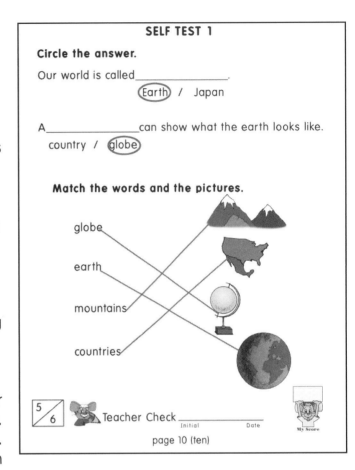

PART II: FRIENDS IN MEXICO

Page 11

CONCEPT: introduction to friends in Mexico

TEACHER GOAL: To teach the children about our neighbor to the South.

READING INTEGRATION: main idea, noting and recalling details, following oral directions

VOCABULARY: (neighbor, Mexico)

MATERIALS NEEDED: yellow and blue crayon, globe, map, picture of Mexican flag

TEACHING PAGE 11:
Use the globe and the wall map to Locate the United States. Have the children find the country that is just south of the United States on the map. Write the word Mexico on the board. Give the children a chance to share anything they may know about the country of Mexico.

Have the children turn to page 11 in the LIFEPAC. Identify the two countries in the picture. Show an enlarged picture of the Mexican flag if one is available. Read the page together. Discuss the meaning of the word *neighbor* in relation to people and what it might mean in relation to whole countries .

ACTIVITY:
Have the children find the words *United States* on the page. Using the blue crayon, tell them to underline the words every time they see them. Have them color the United States in on the map.

Using the yellow crayon, have the children color in the word *Mexico* on the map and underline *Mexico* every time they see the word on page 11.

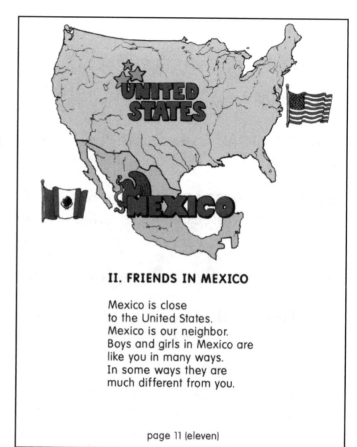

II. FRIENDS IN MEXICO

Mexico is close
to the United States.
Mexico is our neighbor.
Boys and girls in Mexico are
like you in many ways.
In some ways they are
much different from you.

page 11 (eleven)

Pages 12 and 13: Mexico

CONCEPT: the country of Mexico

OBJECTIVE:
I can tell ways all people are alike.
I can tell ways people may be different.
I can tell how people live in Japan and Mexico.

TEACHER GOAL: To teach the children about the land and people of Mexico.

READING INTEGRATION: main idea, noting and recalling details, following written directions, irregular plurals

VOCABULARY: cities, Spanish, English (farmers)

MATERIALS NEEDED: records and books about Mexico that include some Spanish language, map of Mexico, posters and pictures of Mexico and the Mexican people, crayons, Worksheet 3, pencils

TEACHING PAGES 12 and 13:
Show pictures of Mexico and the Mexican people, both city and country people. Read a story such as *Two Pesos for Catalina* by Ann Kirn or *Rosa* by Leo Politi. Any such story will introduce the children to the life of the majority of the Mexican people. It will also give them some idea of the kind of country Mexico is (sand and cactus in the north and hot jungles in the south).

Have the children open their LIFEPACs to page 12. Read the page together. Talk about the concepts presented on the page. Use as many pictures as can be found to help the children visualize the country of Mexico. *Ask questions such as these*:
"What kind of land is in Mexico?
"What do most of the people do?

MEXICO

Mexico is a big country.
It has hot and cool places.
It has dry and rainy places.
Mexico has tall mountains.
Mexico has lots of flat land.
Many people in Mexico
are farmers.
Some people live in cities
and towns.
Most people in Mexico
speak Spanish.

page 12 (twelve)

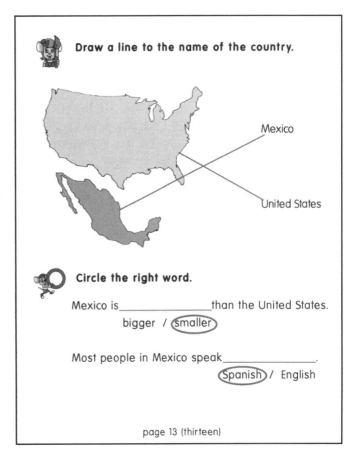

Draw a line to the name of the country.

Mexico

United States

Circle the right word.

Mexico is_____than the United States.
bigger / (smaller)

Most people in Mexico speak_____.
(Spanish) / English

page 13 (thirteen)

153

"What language do the people speak?"
"What kind of place do you see in the picture?"

(Most stories about Mexico include some reference to the marketplace.)

Have the children turn to page 13. Read the directions together. Make sure the children understand what to do before they start to work. After all are finished, correct the page together.

ACTIVITIES:

1.   Have the children underline with a crayon, all the words on page 12 that tell about the country of Mexico.

2.   Introduce the children to some Spanish words that are common in America. These might include *taco, tamale, tostada.* Other Spanish words that the children might enjoy learning are *gracias* (GRAH-see-ahs), thank you; *por favor* (pohr-fah-VOR), please; *buenos dias* (BWAIN-nohs dee-ahs), good morning; *muchacho* (mu-CHA-cho), boy; *muchacha* (mu-CHA-cha), girl; *senor* (sehn-YOR), Mister; *senora* (sehn-YOR-ah), Mrs.; *si* (see), yes; *adios* (ah-dee-YOHS), good-bye.

3.   *Do Worksheet 3.*

Page 12 pictures the market place found in all Mexican villages. The picture on the Worksheet shows a family coming in from the country side to sell their goods. They will also buy the things they need for the coming weeks while at the market. The people are very poor and their needs are quite simple. Many of the things they make are for the tourist trade. The family in the picture is one of the fortunate ones to own a burro. Most of the people carry everything on their backs as they have no animals to do the work. These farmer people raise corn on their very small farms. This is ground to make flour. From this they make tortillas and other corn meal foods. Corn is the main staple in their diets.

Name _____

Discuss the picture and color it.

This Mexican family is on their way to the market place.

History & Geography 109
Worksheet 3
with page 13

Teacher check _____
                    Initial   Date

Discuss the picture with the children. Have pictures available so that the children can see the proper colors for clothing, foods, and so on.

Pages 14 and 15: Carlos

CONCEPT: meet Carlos

OBJECTIVES:
I can tell ways all people are alike.
I can tell ways people may be different.

TEACHER GOALS: To teach the children about life in Mexico City, and about ways Carlos is different from children in the United States and ways he is like children in the United States.

READING INTEGRATION: main idea, noting and recalling details, speaking in a group, listening, dictionary work, following written directions

VOCABULARY: Carlos, soccer, beans, tamales (favorite)

MATERIALS NEEDED: writing tablet, pencils, crayons, drawing paper, electric fry pan, spatula, cooking oil, ingredients for tacos (hamburger, lettuce, cheese, tomatoes, taco sauce)

TEACHING PAGES 14 and 15:

Ask the children to name some of their favorite games and foods. Have them list the things they learn about in school. Make separate lists for each of these categories on the board.

Have the children open the LIFEPACs to pages 14 and 15. Tell the children that the boy on the right is Carlos. The other two boys are his best friends, Juan (in the center) and Jose (on the left). Tell the children to put a red C under the picture of Carlos. Write the names Juan (pronounce the *Ju* as a *w*) and Jose (pronounce the *J* as an *h*) on the board and say them again. Tell the children that some letters of the alphabet have different sounds in other languages. In English, Juan would be John and Jose would be Joseph. Let the children guess what Carlos would be in English (Carl).

CARLOS

Carlos lives in Mexico City.
It is the biggest city in Mexico.
Carlos likes to go to school.
He learns reading and math.
Carlos and his friends play soccer after school.

Carlos is always on time to eat.
Mexican food may be quite different from the food you eat.
Carlos's favorite foods are beans and tamales.

page 14 (fourteen)

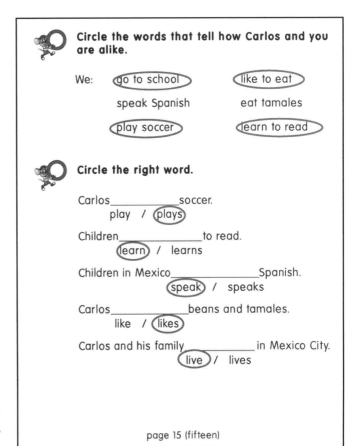

Circle the words that tell how Carlos and you are alike.

We: (go to school)   (like to eat)
     speak Spanish   eat tamales
(play soccer)   (learn to read)

Circle the right word.

Carlos_____ soccer.
    play / (plays)

Children_____ to read.
    (learn) / learns

Children in Mexico_____ Spanish.
    (speak) / speaks

Carlos_____ beans and tamales.
    like / (likes)

Carlos and his family_____ in Mexico City.
    (live) / lives

page 15 (fifteen)

Read the page together. Talk about Carlos' life as compared to the children in the class. Compare the lists of food and games the children made with the food and games Carlos likes. Read the directions on page 15. After the class is finished with the page, check their answers. As you check the first activity, have the children think of other ways that they are like Carlos and some other ways that they are different from Carlos.

ACTIVITIES:

1. Have the children draw a picture showing one way they are different from Carlos. Talk about how differences in people are a gift from God, just as likenesses are. The children should share these pictures with the whole class or in small groups.

2. Try some Mexican foods. Many are available at the grocery store or you can make your own. Tacos would be a simple and delicious way to first try a Mexican-type food. Bean tostadas are also easy to make. For tacos you will need fried out hamburger, crumbled; cheddar cheese, grated; lettuce chopped into small pieces; tomatoes cut into small chunks; taco shells. The taco shell is filled with the above ingredients in layers: hamburger on the bottom and the other ingredients layered on top of it. Top off the whole thing with some taco sauce. (This sauce should be a mild variety if the children have never had it before.)

Bean tostadas are made by spreading heated refried beans (available at the grocery store) on a fried flour or corn tortilla. If left open and flat it is a tostada. If it is rolled up, it is called a bean burro.

3. Tell the children to pretend they are going to write to Carlos and tell him about their favorite food. In their writing tablets, have the children write about two of their favorite foods. Describe what they look like and how they are made.

Pages 16 and 17: Fiesta Time

CONCEPT: holidays in Mexico

OBJECTIVES:
I can tell ways all people are alike.
I can tell ways people may be different.
I can tell how people live in Japan and Mexico.

TEACHER GOAL: To teach the children about several holidays in Mexico and how they are celebrated.

READING INTEGRATION: main idea, noting and recalling details, dictionary work, retelling in own words

VOCABULARY: celebrated, fiestas, Feast, receive, remind, Easter, pinata

MATERIALS NEEDED: crayons, balloons, newspaper, wheat paste or white glue and water, tempera paint, crepe paper, scissors

TEACHING PAGES 16 and 17:

Write the word *fiesta* on the board. Tell the children it is a Spanish word that means party or celebration. The Mexican people have many fiestas. Read books about festivals in Mexico.

Have the children open their LIFEPACs to pages 16 and 17. Read the pages together and discuss them as they are read.

Ask the children:
"What is Carlos' favorite fiesta?"
"What is the Feast of Three Kings?"
"What happens on that day?"
"What is a pinata?"
"What are the children doing in the picture on page 16?"
"What is happening in the picture on page 17?"

FIESTA TIME

Many holidays in Mexico
are celebrated with fiestas.
A fiesta is a party.
Carlos' favorite fiesta time is
the Feast of Three Kings.
On this day, boys and girls
receive gifts.
The gifts remind them of Jesus.
He was God's gift to all people.
Carlos believes in Jesus
as his Saviour.

page 16 (sixteen)

Mexico has many other holidays.
Some of them are Easter,
Independence Day, and
Columbus Day

A <u>pinata</u> filled with candy is
part of every fiesta.

 Color this fiesta picture.

page 17 (seventeen)

ACTIVITIES:

1.   Write the vocabulary words on the board in groups of three or four. Have the children put them in alphabetical order.

2.   *Art Project:* Make a pinata. Let each child make their own simple pinata. Cover blown up balloons with strips of torn newspaper. The newspaper strips are soaked in wheat paste or in a mixture of white glue and water. If glue and water are used the proportions should be no more than one third water to two-thirds glue. When the newspaper is thoroughly dry (about 36 to 48 hrs. drying time), the balloon can be popped with a pin. The outside of the ball can be decorated any way the children want to do it. It can be painted, covered with strips of crepe paper, or colored with other types of decoration. Many books on making pinatas are available from the library.

Pages 18 and 19: Activity Pages

VOCABULARY: floating, gardens

MATERIALS NEEDED: writing tablet, crayons, pencils, number line

TEACHING PAGES 18 and 19:

Write all the vocabulary words on the board from section two. Review them by matching words with meanings. *Example*: Which word tells what language Carlos speaks?

Have the children turn to page 18 in their LIFEPAC. Read the directions together for both activities. Check the first activity when all the children are finished with it.

ACTIVITIES:

1. Have the children share their pictures about favorite holidays with the whole class or in small sharing groups.

2. Have the children write about their favorite holidays in their writing tablets. The stories may be read or put up as part of a bulletin board display.

3. Make statements about the material covered so far in the LIFEPAC. Have the children respond to your statements with the words fact or opinion. This skill may need to be reviewed before asking the children to respond.

Write the answer on the line.

A fiesta is a _party_ .
party / gift

A pinata is filled with _candy_ .
books / candy

Holidays are celebrated with _fiestas_ .
food / fiestas

Carlos lives in _Mexico_ .
Mexico / United States

Draw a picture of your favorite holiday.

page 18 (eighteen)

Follow the dots with a green crayon. Color the picture.

page 19 (nineteen)

Pages 20 and 21: Games and Sports

CONCEPT: games and sports in Mexico

OBJECTIVE: I can tell how people live in Japan and Mexico.

TEACHER GOALS: To teach the children about the games and sports of Mexico, and about one or two games played by Mexican children.

READING INTEGRATION: main idea, noting and recalling details, speaking in a group, listening, following written directions

VOCABULARY: marbles, canicas, hole, point, treat, sport, enjoys, basketball, baseball

MATERIALS NEEDED: small paper cup, aluminum foil, string, marbles, pencils

TEACHING PAGES 20 and 21:

Have the children open their LIFEPACs to page 20. Talk about the picture. Ask if any of the children have ever played a game similar to the one the boys in the picture are playing. Have them explain how to play the game.

Read page 20 together. Discuss the games and sports mentioned on the page. Ask which ones are the same as games in the United States. Ask how the game canicas is played (give several children a chance to explain the game).

Another game often played by Mexican children is *gato y raton* or (*the cat and the mouse.*) This is a circle game played by many children. The children of the class form a circle and hold hands tightly. One child is chosen to be the cat and one the mouse. The mouse is on the inside of the circle. The cat, on the outside, tries to break through the held hands to get to the mouse on the inside. If the cat should break through, he tries to catch the mouse before the mouse

GAMES AND SPORTS

Have you ever played marbles?
Carlos plays a marble game.
It is called <u>canicas</u>.
A small hole is found or made.
One person rolls a marble
into the hole.
If the marble stays in the hole,
you score one point.
Then the next player rolls
his marble.

It is a special treat for Carlos
to go to a soccer game.
This sport is the favorite one
in Mexico.

Other sports that Carlos enjoys
are baseball and basketball.

page 20 (twenty)

Circle the games Carlos likes.

Circle the games you like.

How are children in Mexico and the United States different? How are they the same?

page 21 (twenty-one)

can escape to the outside of the circle. The children in the circle do what they can to keep the cat from catching the mouse. When the mouse is finally caught, a new mouse and cat are chosen.

Read the directions of page 21 together. Discuss the second activity as you check. Have the children explain why they like certain games or sports. Discuss the question at the bottom. List the likenesses and differences on the board as the children give them.

ACTIVITY:

Many children in Mexico play with a small toy called a *valero*. It is a wooden ball with a hole in it. A stick is attached to the ball with a string. The child holds the stick upright, swings the ball up into the air and tries to catch the ball on top of the stick. A similar toy can be made from a paper cup and a small ball made of aluminum foil. Cut a piece of string 8 to 10 inches long and tie a knot on both ends to join the cup and the foil ball. When the cup is held, the ball is swung into the air and caught in the cup on its way down.

Page 22: Self Test 2

CONCEPT: friends of Mexico

OBJECTIVES:
    I can tell ways all people are alike.
    I can tell ways people may be different.
    I can tell how people live in Japan and Mexico.

TEACHER GOAL: To evaluate the children's recall of the material covered in section two.

READING INTEGRATION: recall of details, following written directions, syllables, dictionary work

VOCABULARY: Review all the new words.

MATERIALS NEEDED: vocabulary word cards, pocket chart, pencils

TEACHING PAGE 22:
    Have the children turn to page 22 in their LIFEPACs. Read the directions together. Answer any questions about what to do. Allow the children sufficient time to complete the page. Check the page as soon as possible after all are finished. Allow for family customs on the first activity (some students may celebrate the Feast of Three Kings in their families).

ACTIVITIES:
    1. Put the vocabulary cards in the pocket chart in groups of three or four making sure the first letter of each word in a group is different. Have the children come forward and put the words in each group in alphabetical order. Increase the difficulty by regrouping the words so that the first letters are not all different.

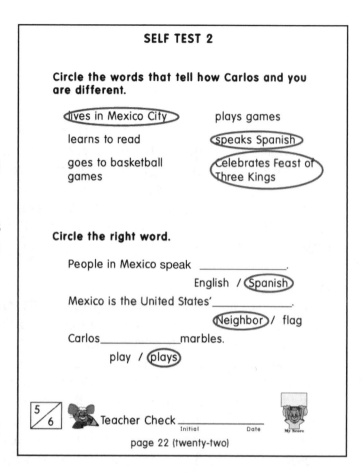

    2. Put all the vocabulary word cards in the pocket chart in random order. Have the children come forward and separate the words into one-syllable, two-syllable, and three-syllable word groups.

PART III: JAPAN

Page 23

CONCEPT: friends in Japan

TEACHER GOAL: To teach the children about some basic geographic facts about the country of Japan.

READING INTEGRATION: main idea, noting and recalling details, following oral directions

VOCABULARY: island

MATERIALS NEEDED: globe, map, crayons, writing tablet, pictures of Japan

TEACHING PAGE 23:

Have the children locate the country of Japan on the globe and on the map. *Ask the children:*

"From the United States which way do you have to go to get to Japan by the shortest route?"

"What ocean is all around Japan?"

"What is land called that has water all around it?"

"How many big islands can you count in the country of Japan?"

Have the children open their LIFEPACs to page 23. Talk about the map and the picture of the flag. Tell the children to color the circle on the flag red. The red ball stands for the rising sun. Japan is often called the land of the rising sun. Have the children put *lines* under the names of the four islands that make up the country of Japan. Tell the children that Japan is a very small country. All the land of Japan is about the same size as the state of California. Locate California on the map. Talk about whether Japan is smaller or larger than the United States.

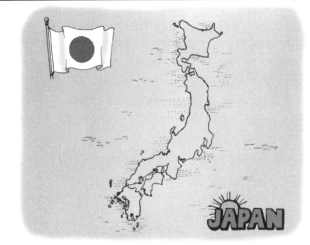

III. FRIENDS IN JAPAN

Japan is far away.
It is across the ocean.
Japan is an island country.
An island has water
all around it.
You will read how children
in Japan are like you.
You will read about ways
they are different from you.

page 23 (twenty-three)

Compare Japan to Mexico and decide which is smaller or larger. Discuss which country, Japan or Mexico, is closer to the United States.

Read page 23 together. Discuss the page.

Ask the children: "What ocean do you have to cross to get to Japan?" (Have the children point to the answer on the map.)

"What is an island?"

"Can you find any other island countries on the map or globe?"

Tell the children to take out a blue crayon. Have them circle the names of the ocean on the map on page 23. With a green crayon, have them underline the word *island* every time you see it on page 23. Have them circle the word *Japan* with a red crayon as often as they find it on the page.

ACTIVITY:

Have the children write several sentences in their writing tablets about what they have learned so far about Japan. Allow time for them to share their sentences with the whole class or in small groups.

Pages 24 and 25: Japan

CONCEPT: more about the land and the people of Japan

OBJECTIVE: I can tell how people live in Japan and Mexico.

TEACHER GOAL: To teach the children about the land of Japan and its people.

READING INTEGRATION: main idea, noting and recalling details, plurals, written directions

VOCABULARY: summer, winter, fishermen

MATERIALS NEEDED: pictures of the land and people of Japan, books about Japan, globe, map, crayons, pencils

TEACHING PAGES 24 and 25:

Have the children come up to the map and point to the countries of Japan, Mexico, and the United States as you name them. Write the names of the three countries on the board. Ask questions about the countries and have different children come up to the board and point to the country that answers the questions.

Show pictures of the land of Japan. Pictures should show the broad variety of countryside in Japan, everything from semitropical forests to the very cold northern areas. Climate variations are similar to those in the United States.

Have the children open their LIFEPACs to page 24. Talk about the picture. Tell the children that the name of the mountain in the picture is Mt. Fuji. Mt. Fuji is very tall and is covered with snow all year round. It is a "sleeping" volcano. It is said to be one of the most beautiful mountains in the world. The Japanese people are very proud of Mt. Fuji. Many people take vacation trips to

JAPAN

Japan is a very small country.
It has many tall mountains.
In summer, Japan is very hot.
In winter it is very cold.
Japan has lots of rain.

Most people live and work
in the cities.
Some people are farmers.
Some people are fisherman.

page 24 (twenty-four)

Color the flags. Write the name of the country.

Japan   Mexico   United States

Mexico

Japan

United States

page 25 (twenty-five)

this mountain every year. Read the page together and discuss it.

Ask the children: "How big is Japan?"

"What is it like in summer?"

"What season of the year has lots of rain?"

"Where do most of the people live and work?"

"What do people do who live out in the country?"

Have the children turn to page 25. Read the directions together. Check the page as soon as all the children are finished. If possible have larger versions of these flags posted on a bulletin board in plain sight of all the children. Review the meaning of the colors and symbols of the flags.

ACTIVITIES:

1.   Have each child draw a picture of a famous landmark in the area in which you live. This landmark should have some national significance. It can be a place of nature (as Mt. Fuji in Japan) or a man made landmark. (Mt. Rushmore, for instance). After they are finished with their pictures, allow time for the children to share their work with the whole class or in small sharing groups.

2.   Have them write in their writing tablets about the kind of work done by the children's parents. Compare with what is known about work done by people in Japan.

3.   Read a story about living in the country in Japan. Read other stories that tell about the life of different people in the country.

Pages 26 and 27: Ikuko

CONCEPT: Ikuko

OBJECTIVE: I can tell how people live in Japan and Mexico.

READING INTEGRATION: main idea, noting and recalling details, following written directions

VOCABULARY: Ikuko, paper, wood, music

MATERIALS NEEDED: crayons, string, scissors, Worksheets 4 and 5, paste, pictures of Japanese people

TEACHING PAGES 26 and 27:
    Show the children pictures of Japanese people, cities, houses, and so on.
    Discuss the illustration on page 26.
    Read the text on pages 26 and 27.
    Ask the children:
    "Where does Ikuko live?"
    "What is her house made of?"
    "How many days does she go to school?"
    "What does she learn in school?"
    "What does Ikuko do after school?"
    "What is the Japanese favorite sport?"
    Read the direction sentence. When the children finish their drawings, let them share them with the class.

ACTIVITIES:
    1.   Worksheet 4 is a mobile for the children to put together and hang up to remind them that people all over the world are their friends and neighbors. To make the mobile more durable, the children might glue all the pieces to cardboard before they string them together. Hang the finished mobiles around the room until the LIFEPAC has been completed.
    2.   Introduce the children to the art of Japanese paper folding or *origami.* Using the basic outline on Worksheet 5, the

IKUKO

Ikuko lives in a small city.
Her house is made
of paper and wood.
She goes to school
six days a week.
She learns reading, writing,
spelling, and math.
She learns music and art.
She learns about Jesus.

page 26 (twenty-six)

After school, Ikuko plays
in the park with her friends.
Sometimes, she goes
to a baseball game.
Baseball is the favorite sport
of Japanese people.

 Draw a picture showing what you like to do after school.

page 27 (twenty-seven)

children can make a folded replica of a volcano. This replica can then be used as part of a picture, either painted or drawn, of Mt. Fuji or another famous volcano. All folding directions are on the Worksheet (The pattern should be duplicated onto regular weight typing paper).

Name _____

World Friends Mobile

FRIENDS AROUND
THE
WORLD

Directions
Color pictures.
Cut out pictures.
Tie pictures with
string as in the picture.

History & Geography 109
Worksheet 4
with page 27

Teacher check _____
Initial   Date

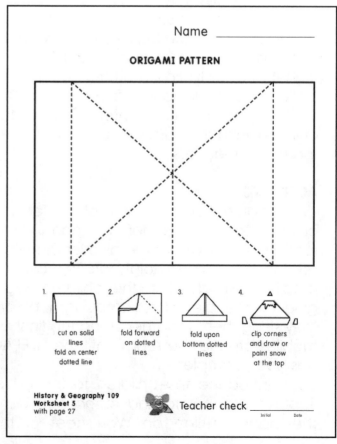

Name _____

ORIGAMI PATTERN

1.	2.	3.	4.
cut on solid lines fold on center dotted line	fold forward on dotted lines	fold upon bottom dotted lines	clip corners and draw or paint snow at the top

History & Geography 109
Worksheet 5
with page 27

Teacher check _____
Initial   Date

Page 28 and 29: Two Ways of Living

CONCEPT: two ways of living

OBJECTIVE: I can tell how people live in Japan and Mexico.

TEACHER GOAL: To teach the children the idea of people living and working in a dual culture.

READING INTEGRATION: main idea, noting and recalling details, following written directions, writing sentences

VOCABULARY: Japanese, English, clothes, kimono, getas, furniture, table, pillows, vegetables

MATERIALS NEEDED: Worksheet 6, crayons, pictures that show the traditional way of living and the modern, western living in Japan, pencils

TEACHING PAGES 28 and 29:

Use the pictures to compare the way people live in Japan. Many of the books about Japan point out the modern and traditional ways. For instance, a man might wear a Western style suit to work every day, but as soon as he gets home he will change into the traditional kimono. This custom is true for many Japanese people. In their social life, the people may go to sports events and picnics, but the traditional entertainment such as kabuki plays and sumo wrestling are just as popular. Compare living in Japan with life in the United States where you live.

Have the children open their LIFEPACs to pages 28 and 29. Read the pages together and talk about them

Ask the children:

"What languages does Ikuko learn?"
"What is a kimono?" "What are getas?"
"What are the main foods in Japan?"

TWO WAYS OF LIVING

Ikuko learns two ways of living.
She learns Japanese and English in school.
Sometimes she wears clothes just like yours.
For special days she wears a <u>kimono</u> and <u>getas</u>.

page 28 (twenty-eight)

Ikuko's home has
little furniture.
Her family eats at a low table.
They sit on pillows.
They eat rice, fish, and vegetables.
Ikuko sleeps on a soft mat.
In the daytime she rolls it up

Ikuko and her family are at dinner.

 Color the picture.

page 29 (twenty-nine)

169

"What is Ikuko's bed like?"

"Why do you think Ikuko rolls up her bed in the daytime?"

Explain to the children as they work on the picture on page 29, that the Japanese people who live in the old style wood and paper houses have little furniture. The reason for this is that heavy furniture would destroy the tatami mats that mat up the floors in these Japanese homes. For this same reason, a person always removes street shoes before going into the house.

ACTIVITIES:

1.   Read a story about a Japanese boy or girl and the way they live. Use the story as the basis for a discussion. The discussion may be held in small groups or with the class as a whole.

2.   Worksheet 6 may be used as a worksheet or you may write the questions on the board and have the children answer them in their writing tablets.

3.   Build models of the kind of homes in which Carlos and Ikuko live. You will need clay for a Mexican home. Popsicle sticks or toothpicks covered with tissue paper would make good Japanese homes. Boxes painted appropriately might also be used. The children might also want to make models of their own homes to display along with those of Carlos and Ikuko.

Name _____

Write a sentence telling where Ikuko lives.

(Japan)

How many days a week do you go to school?

(5)

Write a sentence tell about the house in which you live.

(will vary)

History & Geography 109
Worksheet 6
with page 29

Teacher check _____
Initial   Date

Pages 30 and 31: Japanese Holidays

CONCEPTS: holidays in Japan

OBJECTIVE: I can tell how people live in Japan and Mexico.

TEACHER GOAL: To teach the children several important Japanese holidays and their significance.

READING INTEGRATION: main idea, noting and recalling details, following written directions

VOCABULARY: decorations, Festival, cloth, flown

MATERIALS NEEDED: Worksheet 7, crayons, large size construction paper or tissue paper in assorted colors, scissors, glue, writing tablet, pencils

TEACHING PAGES 30 and 31:

Have the children open their LIFEPACs to pages 30 and 31. Talk about what they see in the picture. Read the page together. *Ask the children*: "What is the holiday that is represented in the picture?" Explain to the children that until recently very few Christian holidays were celebrated in Japan because there were very few Christian people. That is changing today. Ikuko, as a Christian, celebrates Christmas, Easter, and other Christian holidays just like we do. Finish reading the top of page 31.

Ask:

"Do people in the United States have any holidays just for children?"

"What groups of people do we honor with special holidays?"

(Mothers' Day, Fathers' Day, Grandparents' Day)

Complete and check the activity on page 31. Look up any answers that cause difficulty.

HOLIDAYS IN JAPAN

Ikuko has two favorite holidays.
The most exciting one is New Years.
Everyone puts up decorations.
Mother makes special foods.
People give gifts to each other.

The Festival of Dolls is
a special day for girls.
Ikuko invites her friends
to a party.

page 30 (thirty)

Another holiday is Boys' Day.
A cloth fish is flown in honor
of each boy in a family.
Most of Japan's holidays are
much different than yours.

 Circle yes or no.

Ikuko learns Japanese and Spanish in school.
yes (no)

Ikuko sits on a chair when she eats.
yes (no)

Ikuko learns two ways of living.
(yes) no

Ikuko has a party on the Festival of Dolls.
(yes) no

On New Years, Mother makes special foods.
(yes) no

page 31 (thirty-one)

ACTIVITIES:

1. Worksheet 7 gives the children an idea what the carp kite flown on Boys' Day looks like. The carp is a symbol of strength and determination to the Japanese people. Boys' Day is an opportunity for fathers to share with their sons stories of national heroes of Japan.

2. Have the children write about an American holiday that is not celebrated in Japan. The story could be in the form of a letter to Ikuko, telling her about the celebration here.

3. Make a carp kite similar to the ones flown in Japan. These may be made two or three-dimensional. A two-dimensional fish can be drawn on construction paper, decorated, and cut out. If a three-dimensional fish is made, cut out two identical fish patterns. Lay them together and decorate both sides. After the fish have been decorated, glue them carefully together along the edge of the patterns. Leave an opening at the mouth. The fish may be lightly stuffed with crumpled newspaper or other scrap paper. These fish can then be flown from sticks or hung as mobiles.

Name _____

Color and discuss the picture.

Boys' Day in Japan

History & Geography 109
Worksheet 7
with page 31

Teacher check _____
Initial   Date

Pages 32: Activity Page

MATERIALS NEEDED: pencils, globe, map

TEACHING PAGE 32:

Review the concepts taught about the land and people of Japan. Use the globe and world map and have the children point out where the country is located. Ask questions about what the country is like. Put up pictures of Japan and Mexico and have the children tell which are the pictures of Japan. Compare Mexico and Japan with the United States and decide which land is more like our country.

Discuss likenesses and differences between Japanese people and people in the United States and in Mexico. List these differences and likenesses by country. Talk about the lists. In general, the same likenesses show up no matter what people of the world are being considered. Relate the whole discussion to the Biblical truth that all people are created the same on the inside. It is only in some outward ways that people differ from each other.

Have the children open their LIFEPACs to page 32. Read the directions together. Check the page as soon as all the children are finished. At this point take time to review parts one and two of this LIFEPAC in preparation for the self test and LIFEPAC Test.

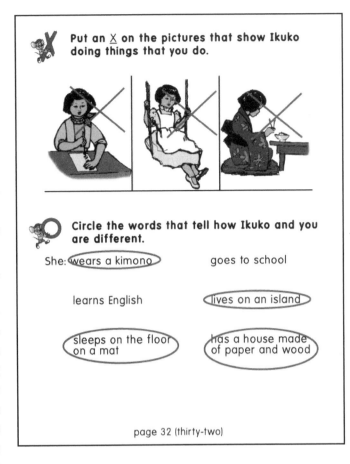

Page 33: Self Test 3

CONCEPT: evaluation

OBJECTIVES:

I can tell about a globe.
I can tell ways all people are alike.
I can tell ways people may be different.
I can tell how people live in Japan and Mexico.

READING INTEGRATION: following written directions, recalling details

VOCABULARY: Review all the vocabulary

MATERIALS NEEDED: pencils, writing tablet

TEACHING PAGE 33:

Have the children turn to page 33 in the LIFEPAC. Read the directions together. Answer any questions about what to do. Identify all illustrations. Allow the children sufficient time to complete the page. Check the page as soon as possible after all are finished.

ACTIVITIES

1. Review all the vocabulary words learned in this LIFEPAC. Use the pocket chart to post the words in groups of about ten. Say a word and have a child come up and take that word from the chart. Replace the word and follow the same procedure with all the words.

Go through the words a second time. This time, give a definition for one of the words and ask a child to find that word.

2. Have the children write a paragraph in their writing tablets about each country they have learned about, including their own. They might just tell about the land or the people or about the likenesses and differences in people of different countries.

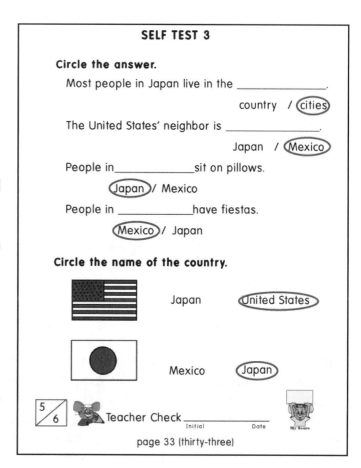

SELF TEST 3

Circle the answer.

Most people in Japan live in the _____.
country / (cities)

The United States' neighbor is _____.
Japan / (Mexico)

People in_____sit on pillows.
(Japan)/ Mexico

People in _____have fiestas.
(Mexico)/ Japan

Circle the name of the country.

Japan   (United States)

Mexico   (Japan)

5/6   Teacher Check _____
Initial   Date

page 33 (thirty-three)

LIFEPAC TEST AND ALTERNATE LIFEPAC TEST

Administer the test to the class as a group. Ask to have directions read or read them to the class. In either case, be sure that the children clearly understand. Put examples on the board if it seems necessary. Give ample time for each activity to be completed before going to the next.

Correct immediately and discuss with the child.

Review any concepts that have been missed.

Give those children who do not achieve the 80% score additional copies of the worksheets and a list of vocabulary words to study. A parent of a classroom helper should help in the review.

When the child is ready, give the Alternate LIFEPAC Test. Use the same procedure as for the LIFEPAC TEST.

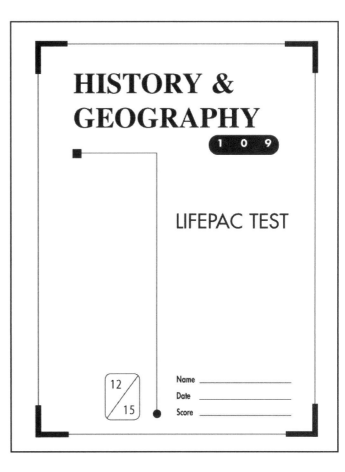

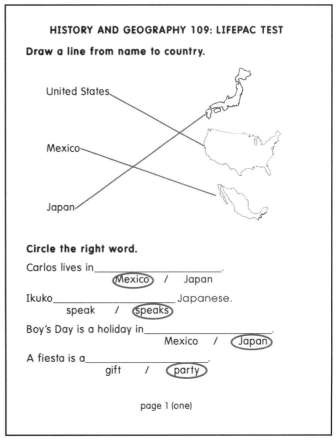

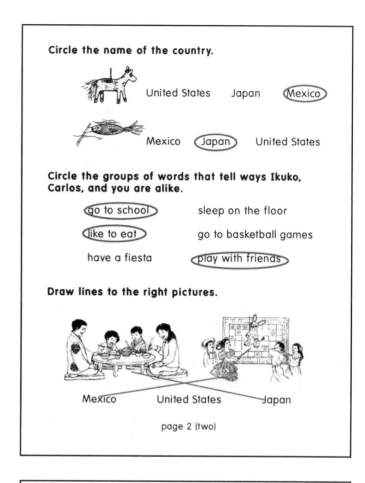

Circle the name of the country.

United States   Japan   (Mexico)

Mexico   (Japan)   United States

Circle the groups of words that tell ways Ikuko, Carlos, and you are alike.

(go to school)   sleep on the floor

(like to eat)   go to basketball games

have a fiesta   (play with friends)

Draw lines to the right pictures.

Mexico   United States   Japan

page 2 (two)

NOTES

page 3 (three)

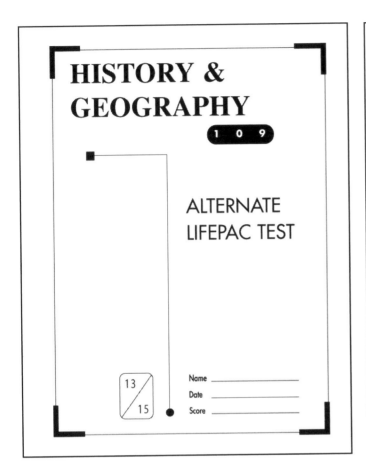

HISTORY & GEOGRAPHY

1 0 9

ALTERNATE LIFEPAC TEST

13/15

Name _____

Date _____

Score _____

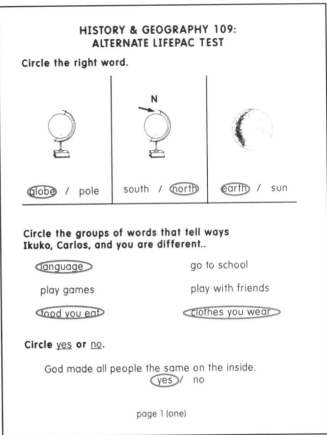

**HISTORY & GEOGRAPHY 109:
ALTERNATE LIFEPAC TEST**

Circle the right word.

globe / pole | south / north | earth / sun

**Circle the groups of words that tell ways
Ikuko, Carlos, and you are different..**

language   go to school

play games   play with friends

food you eat   clothes you wear

Circle yes or no.

God made all people the same on the inside.
yes / no

page 1 (one)

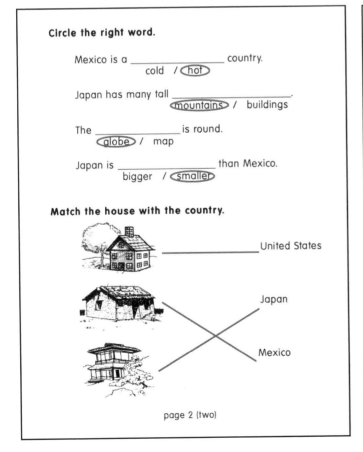

Circle the right word.

Mexico is a _____ country.
cold / hot

Japan has many tall _____.
mountains / buildings

The _____ is round.
globe / map

Japan is _____ than Mexico.
bigger / smaller

Match the house with the country.

United States

Japan

Mexico

page 2 (two)

NOTES

page 3 (three)

Page 1: The World and You

CONCEPT: the world and you

OBJECTIVE: To introduce all the objectives.

TEACHER GOAL: To teach the children what a review LIFEPAC is.

READING INTEGRATION: table of contents, main idea, noting and recalling details, retelling in own words, writing sentences

MATERIALS NEEDED: writing tablet, magazines, glue, scissors, construction paper, drawing paper, pencils

TEACHING PAGE 1:

Have the children read the title of the LIFEPAC. Explain that this is the last LIFEPAC at this level and that it will review all the things they have learned throughout the 100 level of social studies. Open the book to the contents. Have the children tell you what a contents page is. Go through the contents and locate titles and page numbers. Have the children tell about each of the headings. Questions will help to refresh their memories.

Turn to page 1. Discuss the picture in light of the title. *Ask:* "What is the meaning of the picture?" Read the page together. As you read each sentence, have the children respond with anything they remember about that subject.

ACTIVITIES:

1. Have the children write sentences in their writing tablets about the various headings on the contents page. Have them make illustrations to go with the sentences.

2. Have each child draw a picture of himself and cut it out. Have him glue this self-portrait in the middle of a piece of construction paper. Then have the children look through magazines to find pictures of

THE WORLD AND YOU

You have studied much
about yourself this year.
You have studied
about other people.
You have studied about the world
in which you live.

 Objectives

1. I can tell about myself.
2. I can tell about people who live around me.
3. I can tell about the world in which I live.

page 1 (one)

things in the world around them that they especially like or that are especially meaningful to them. These pictures should be glued all around the cutout of themselves. Use these collages as a bulletin board display to introduce this LIFEPAC.

Pages 2 and 3: Activity Pages

VOCABULARY: Review of vocabulary words from LIFEPACs 101, 102, and 103.

MATERIALS NEEDED: word cards, pocket chart, writing tablet, crayons, pencils

TEACHING PAGES 2 and 3:

Have the children turn to page 2 in their LIFEPACs. Read the directions together. Tell the children that some things are missing from the picture. You are going to tell them to draw some of the missing parts. They are to draw only what you tell them in just the way you tell them. Stress the importance of following the directions exactly as you give them.

1. Add a star over the stable.
2. Color the star yellow.
3. Draw a lamb near the manger.
4. Draw Mary to the *right* of the manger. Color her dress blue.
5. Draw Joseph to the *left* of the manger. Color his robe brown.

When the children have finished coloring the rest of the picture any way they choose, break into small discussion groups. Have each group talk about the question at the bottom of the page. After five or ten minutes, come together again and have each group share what the picture "said" to them.

As a follow-up activity, have the children write a story in their writing tablets to go with the picture.

Have the children turn to page 3. Read the directions together. Give the children sufficient time to complete the page. Check the page as soon as all are finished.

ACTIVITY:

Review all the vocabulary words from the first three social studies LIFEPACs. This review can be done with flashcards or by writing the words on the board. Have the children just read the words the first time through. On the second time, have them tell what the words mean or use them in sentences.

Color the picture and talk about it.

What does the picture tell about you and the world.

page 2 (two)

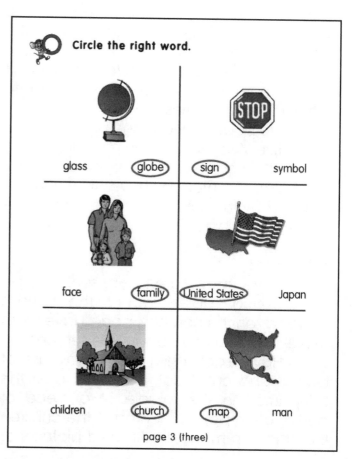

Circle the right word.

glass   (globe)   (sign)   symbol

face   (family)   (United States)   Japan

children   (church)   (map)   man

page 3 (three)

PART I. ALL ABOUT YOU

Pages 4 and 5

CONCEPT: all about you

OBJECTIVE: I can tell about myself.

TEACHER GOAL: To review the LIFEPAC about the child and other people around him.

READING INTEGRATION: main idea, noting and recalling details, writing a story, speaking in front of a group, following written directions

VOCABULARY: (special, person, wonderful, body, feelings)

MATERIALS NEEDED: writing tablet, pencils

TEACHING PAGES 4 and 5:

Write the vocabulary words on the board. These are words that should be especially emphasized in section one of the LIFEPAC. Have the children read the words. Talk about what they mean. Use them in sentences.

Read page 4 together. Talk about what being a special person means. Have the children tell some things about their bodies that they consider wonderful.

Look at the pictures on the top of page 5. Have someone read the discussion question. Give the children a few minutes to look at the pictures. As the children mention likenesses and differences list them on the board. Make a point to stress to the children that in one important way all people are alike, they are created and loved by God.

Finish page 5 and check the page when all the children are finished.

I. ALL ABOUT YOU

God made you because
He loves you.
You are a special person.
You are different
from any other person.
God gave you a wonderful body.
God gave you feelings.
You show your love for God
by taking care of yourself.

page 4 (four)

 Talk about how these children are alike and how they are different.

 **Circle the right word.**

God_____ you.
love / (loves)

You_____ God for your body.
(thank) / thanks

Children_____ at the park.
(play) / plays

page 5 (five)

181

ACTIVITIES:

1.   Have the children write a story in their writing tablets about "How I Take Care of Myself. " Allow time for the children to share their stories.

2.   Hold a special Primary Olympics designed to show that each child is a special person. Include academic subjects, sports, game activities, and such things as art, music, and dramatics. Stress that in this olympic contest there will be no winners. Each person must participate in some way. All the activities combined will make a nice program for the parents. The children should all understand that the purpose of this program is to show how everyone has some special area in which they excel. You, as teacher, must make sure that activities will include the best points of every child in the class.

Pages 6 and 7: You are a Special Person

CONCEPT: You are a special person.

OBJECTIVE: I can tell about myself.

TEACHER GOAL: To review the ways that all people are special.

READING INTEGRATION: main idea, noting and recalling details, following written directions, speaking in a group

VOCABULARY: (family, answers, prayers)

MATERIALS NEEDED: writing tablet, drawing paper, crayons, pencils

TEACHING PAGES 6 and 7:

Write the vocabulary words on the board. Without saying them first, say definitions for each word and have a child identify the word you are talking about. Have other children use the words in sentences.

Turn to page 6 in the LIFEPAC and read the page together. Have the children find the three vocabulary words that are on the board in the book and circle them. After reading the page, ask the children to tell what makes them special persons. Talk about ways people show their thanks to God for His love.

Now have the children look at page 7. Read the directions together. Give the children time to complete both activities before checking the page. Talk about each answer as the page is checked. Ask the children to explain why they chose certain answers and not others.

ACTIVITIES:

1. Have the children write a prayer in their writing tablets thanking God for making them special and for sending Jesus so they can live with Him forever in heaven. Have them share their prayers with their families.

YOU ARE A SPECIAL PERSON

God made you a special person.
You have your own family.
Your name tells who you are.
No other person looks
just like you.

God loves you.
He takes care of you.
He answers your prayers.
You show love for God
when you are kind and helpful.
You show your love for God
when you thank Him
for sending Jesus.

page 6 (six)

Circle the right answer.

You are special because_____
loves you.   Mother / Father / God

You are_____ anyone else.
      different from / the same as

When you act like a special person, you
show good_____.
          health / manners

Circle the picture of the child who shows love for Jesus.

page 7 (seven)

2. Draw pictures of families. Write several sentences about each family member. Share the sentences and pictures with the class.

3. Have each child draw a picture of himself and a best friend. Emphasize external differences such as coloring, dress, length of hair, and so on. Write the name of the friend under the picture. The picture should show how the two children are different. Have each child write a paragraph about how he/she is like the friend that he/she drew. Share the paragraphs and pictures with the class.

Pages 8 and 9: Let's Communicate

CONCEPT: let's communicate

OBJECTIVE: I can tell about people who live around me.

TEACHER GOALS:
To review the many ways people and other living creatures communicate with each other.

How people who are *hearing* or *sight* impaired learn to communicate with other people.

READING INTEGRATION: main idea, noting and recalling details, following written directions, writing sentences, dictionary work, classifying

VOCABULARY: (communication, communicate, sound, voices, sirens, praises, silently, maps, smile)

MATERIALS NEEDED: magazines, glue, writing tablet, scissors, Worksheet 1, word cards, pencils, pocket chart

TEACHING PAGES 8 and 9:
Place all the vocabulary word cards in the pocket chart. Separate them into groups of three or four. Have the children read them as they rearrange them in alphabetical order. Give definitions for some of the words and ask individual children to select the correct word and hand it to you. Ask another child to use the word in a sentence.

Have the children open their LIFEPACs to page 8. Read the page together. Discuss the page as it is read. Ask the children to name as many ways as they can think of to communicate. After they are listed, group them according to sound or silent communication. Talk about hearing-impaired people. Review the ways in which

LET'S COMMUNICATE

Telling someone something is communication.
There are many ways to communicate.
You can communicate with sound.
People's voices and sirens are sounds that communicate.
We communicate with God when we sing praises and pray to Him.
You can communicate silently.
Maps show you where to go.
A smile tells someone you are happy.

page 8 (eight)

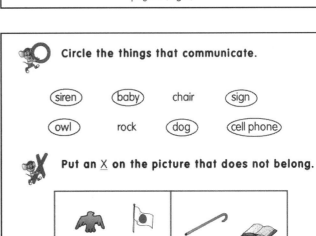

Circle the things that communicate.

siren   baby   chair   sign

owl   rock   dog   cell phone

Put an X on the picture that does not belong.

page 9 (nine)

they communicate with other people. Also review the ways in which blind people communicate, especially the way in which they cope with silent communication signals in the world around them. Reread the sections in Social Studies LIFEPAC 102 that deal with blind and deaf people and how they communicate.

Have the children turn to page 9. Read the directions together. Give the children sufficient time to complete the entire page. Check the page together as soon as all the children are finished.

ACTIVITIES:

1. Practice giving and receiving silent communication signals by body language.

2. Have the children find two or three pictures of any form of communication. Glue these down the left side of a piece of writing tablet paper. Next to each picture, have the children write several sentences about the picture. Share these with the class when there is time. They may be posted as a bulletin board display.

3. Worksheet 1 will review the children's recognition and understanding of some of the vocabulary words presented in section one. Read the directions with the children and do the first one or two with them. They should be able to finish the page independently.

Name _____

Write the number of the word next to the right sentence.

1. communicate   4. sound
2. special   5. silent
3. feelings   6. family

__6__ You are part of these.

__2__ This is the way each person is to God.

__3__ When you cry, you show these.

__1__ You do this when you call someone on the telephone.

__5__ This is the way the world seems to a deaf person.

__4__ When you sing, you make this.

History & Geography 110
Worksheet 1
with page 9

Teacher check _____
                  Initial   Date

Pages 10 and 11: You Have Feelings

CONCEPT: You have feelings.

OBJECTIVE: I can tell about myself.

TEACHER GOAL: To teach the children that all people have feelings given to us by God.

READING INTEGRATION: main idea, noting and recalling details, following written directions, speaking in a group, following oral directions, listening

VOCABULARY: (afraid, angry, share)

MATERIALS NEEDED: pencils, tempera paint, crayons, 9" x 12" paper for painting, word cards, lunch-size paper sacks, pictures of clowns

TEACHING PAGES 10 and 11:

Have the children open their LIFEPACs to page 10. Have the children read the page orally. Talk about the pictures in connection with the text of the page. Tell the children they are going to mark some of the pictures in a certain way. Give the following directions:

1. *Circle* the happy face.
2. Put a *one* above the angry face.
3. Put a *box* around the sad face.
4. Color the hair *yellow* on the girl who is scared.

Write the words *happy, sad, afraid,* and *angry* on the board. Read these words or have a child read them. Have the children turn to page 11 and read the directions. Check the page when all the children have finished. If any of the pictures are interpreted differently than the answers in the Teacher Handbook, have that child explain his or her reasoning. In such cases, it is entirely up to the teacher whether the answer is correct.

YOU HAVE FEELINGS

God gave you feelings.
Sometimes you feel happy.
Sometimes you feel sad.
You may feel afraid or angry.
God wants you to share
your feelings with Him.
He will help when
you are sad or afraid.
When you are happy,
God shares your happiness.

page 10 (ten)

Write how the children feel. Use these words.

happy   sad   afraid   angry

afraid   sad

angry   happy

page 11 (eleven)

ACTIVITIES:

1.   Have the children act out various situations involving strong feelings. The teacher should suggest these situations, at least at first.

2.   Show as many pictures of clowns as possible. Talk about why clowns wear such faces. When a clown is in makeup, can you tell how he really feels or do you just see the madeup face? The makeup covers up the real face and the real feelings. Sometimes people are just like clowns. They cover up their real feelings by putting on a false face. Sometimes this is the only way to behave and sometimes it can be the wrong thing to do. Talk about when it would be good to let your real feelings show and in what situations it might be best to cover up your feelings, at least for a time.

After the discussion, pass out the paper and the paints. Let each child create their own clown face. Encourage them to use bright colors and large designs.

Page 12 : Self Test

CONCEPT: all about you

OBJECTIVE: I can tell about myself.

TEACHER GOAL: To evaluate the children's responses to the self test.

READING INTEGRATION: recalling details, following written directions, speaking in a group, listening, retelling in own words

VOCABULARY: Review all the words.

MATERIALS NEEDED: lunch-size paper sacks, Worksheet 2, crayons, yarn and other scraps to decorate the puppets, construction paper, pencils

TEACHING PAGE 12:

Have the children turn to page 32 in their LIFEPACs. Read the directions together. Answer any questions about what to do. Identify all the illustrations. Allow the children sufficient time to complete the page. Check the page as soon as possible after all are finished.

ACTIVITY:

Pass out Worksheet 2 and the paper sacks. Have the children illustrate the puppet face with a very definite expression of feeling. Attach the face to the bottom of the sack as in the illustration. Add all the finishing details with yarn, cloth, cotton, and so on. Use the puppets to play out various situations calling for emotional responses.

PART II. PEOPLE AROUND US

Page 13

CONCEPT: people around us

OBJECTIVE: I can tell about people who live around me.

TEACHER GOAL: To teach the children about some of the important people in the children's lives.

READING INTEGRATION: main idea, noting and recalling details, writing sentences

VOCABULARY: (neighbors)

MATERIALS NEEDED: writing tablet, pencils

TEACHING PAGE 13:

Write the words PEOPLE AROUND US on the board. Ask the children what those words make them think of. Have them name some of the people who are around them. Talk about how these people affect the lives of the children and their families.

Have the children open their LIFEPACs to page 13. Read the page silently.

Ask: "Who puts other people and helpers into your life?"

"Who did God give you to take care of you as you grow up?"

"Who are some special helpers who keep you well?"

"Name some helpers who teach you about God's love."

ACTIVITY:

Tell the children to make a list of helpers in their lives. Then have them choose the five most important ones to them. Write two sentences about why each one of these friends or helpers is important to the child. Share the sentences with the class.

II. PEOPLE AROUND US

God puts many people
into your life.
He gave you your own
special family.
You have friends and neighbors.

God gives you special helpers
to keep you safe.
Other helpers keep you well and
help you learn.

page 13 (thirteen)

Pages 14 and 15: Your Family

CONCEPT: your family

OBJECTIVE: I can tell about people who live around me.

TEACHER GOAL: To help the children gain a deeper understanding of family relationships.

READING INTEGRATION: main idea, noting and recalling details, following written directions, speaking in a group, listening

MATERIALS NEEDED: crayons, chart paper

TEACHING PAGES 14 and 15:

Have the children open their LIFEPACs to page 14. Talk about the picture and read the title. *Ask* "Are the cat and dog really members of the family?" Read the page together. Talk about some Bible families such as Joseph's and David's. Talk about how they helped each other. Encourage the children to talk about ways their families help each other.

Have the children draw pictures of their families on page 15. Remind them to show the size differences between members as well as other less obvious differences.

ACTIVITIES:

1. Have each child tell about the picture he drew.
2. Make a graph showing the number of persons in the children's families. When the graph is finished, use the graph to answer questions about the biggest and smallest size families.

YOUR FAMILY

Families live together.
They work together.
They play together.
God wants families
to help each other.
All families are not
the same size.
How big is your family?

page 14 (fourteen)

Draw a picture of your family playing together.

page 15 (fifteen)

Pages 16 and 17: Your School and Church

CONCEPT: your school and church

OBJECTIVE: I can tell about people who live around me.

TEACHER GOAL: To review with the children the friends who work for the school and the church.

READING INTEGRATION: main idea, noting and recalling details, following written directions

VOCABULARY: (important, principal, classmates, teachers, secretary, pastor, congregation, worship)

MATERIALS NEEDED: writing tablet, pencils

TEACHING PAGES 16 and 17:

Have the children open their LIFEPACs to pages 16 and 17. Talk about the people in the picture. Discuss who they are and how they help the children. Read page 16 together. Talk about the members of your school family. List them on the board. Ask the children if they think all school families are just alike.

Go on to page 17 and read the paragraph together. Ask the children to share about the people who make up their church families. List these on the board. Complete the activity on page 17 and check it when all the children are finished.

ACTIVITIES:

1. Have the children choose two persons from each list you made on the board. Have them write a paragraph about each of the people they chose from the list. Read the paragraphs when time allows.

2. Have the children write thank you letters to the people they wrote about thanking them for the work they do in the church and the school .

YOUR SCHOOL AND CHURCH

Going to school is very important.
You have many friends in school.
The teachers, principal,
classmates, and secretary are
all part of the school family.
They help you learn how
to show love for Jesus
by loving others.
In school we have times for work
and times for play.

page 16 (sixteen)

Your pastor is the head
of your church family.
He leads the congregation
in worshipping God.
Going to church is
a very special time.
It is a way of saying to God,
"I love you."

 Match the words with the pictures.

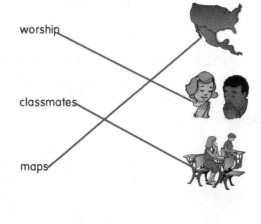

worship

classmates

maps

page 17 (seventeen)

Pages 18 and 19: Activity Pages

MATERIALS NEEDED: drawing paper, construction paper, scissors, glue, crayons, magazines, pencils

TEACHING PAGES 18 and 19:

Have the children turn to page 18. Read the first three lines. Talk about the kinds of food that are considered good food and what would be poor food. Talk about why we need food and what happens to the body when it does not get the right kind of food or enough of the right kind of food. Show pictures of many foods cut from magazines and decide as a class whether each one would be considered good food or poor food. Sometimes the quantity of a certain food that is consumed determines whether it is good or poor food.

Have the children complete the activities on pages 18 and 19. Check the answers together. Discuss the questions as they are being checked.

ACTIVITY:

Have each child show what is a good breakfast by cutting shapes of food from construction paper and pasting them down, collage style, on another piece of paper. When the children have their breakfast pictures finished, have each child share why his picture shows a good breakfast.

God gives us good food to eat.
It helps us do our work.
It gives us energy to play.

Write 1, 2, 3 to show what happens first, second, and third.

Circle the child who ate a good breakfast.

What is a good breakfast?

page 18 (eighteen)

Match the people with the places.

page 19 (nineteen)

Pages 20 and 21: Community Helpers

CONCEPT: community helpers

OBJECTIVE: I can tell about people who live around me.

TEACHER GOAL: To review with the children the role of community helpers in their lives.

READING INTEGRATION: main idea, noting and recalling details, following written directions, classification

VOCABULARY: (community, dentists, listening, doctors, policemen, minister)

MATERIALS NEEDED: writing tablet, pencils

TEACHING PAGES 20 and 21:

Have the children open their LIFEPACs to page 20. *Discuss the pictures.* "Who are the people in the picture and what do they do to help the people who live in the community?" *Discuss the meaning of the word community.* "What other community helpers are there besides the ones pictured on the page?"

Read the page together. Give the children a chance to share personal experiences with the various helpers.

Have the children read the directions at the top of page 21. Check the page as soon as the children are finished.

ACTIVITY:

Tell the children to choose one community helper that they might like to be like when they grow up. Have them write a story about what it would be like to be a _____. Have them share their stories.

COMMUNITY HELPERS

A community is a town or city.
Your community has many helpers.
Some helpers, like firemen and
policemen, keep you safe.
Doctors and dentists help you
stay well.
Your minister and teacher help
you learn.
God gives you all of these helpers.
He wants you to help them
by listening to them and
by obeying them.

page 20 (twenty)

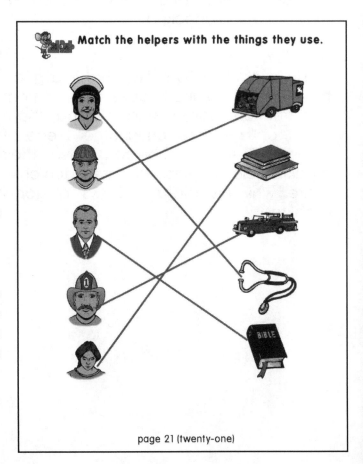

Match the helpers with the things they use.

page 21 (twenty-one)

Page 22: Activity Page

MATERIALS NEEDED: pencils

TEACHING PAGE 22:

Review the jobs of community helpers. Have the children open their LIFEPACs to page 22. Read the directions together. Check the page as soon as the children are finished.

Review all the vocabulary words from section two of the LIFEPAC. Use the word chart or word cards and the pocket chart. Make sure the children not only recognize the words, but that they also can read them and know what they mean.

 Circle the name of the helper.

Who puts out fires?

dentist / (fireman)

Who keeps you safe in the park?

(policeman) / city worker

Who teaches you God's Word?

librarian / (minister)

Who helps you stay well?

teacher / (doctor)

Who keeps your city clean?

(city worker) / fireman

page 22 (twenty-two)

Page 23: Self Test 2

CONCEPT: evaluation

OBJECTIVE: I can tell about people who live around me.

READING INTEGRATION: following written directions, recalling details

VOCABULARY: Review all the words.

MATERIALS NEEDED: pencils

TEACHING PAGE 23:

Have the children turn to page 23 in the LIFEPACs. Read the directions together. Answer any questions about what to do. Identify all illustrations. Allow the children sufficient time to complete the page. Check the page as soon as possible after all are finished. Review any concepts missed.

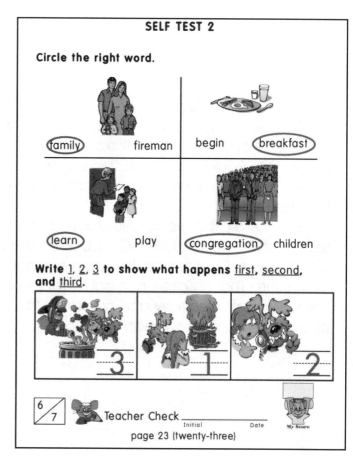

196

PART III. THE WORLD AROUND YOU

Pages 24 and 25

CONCEPT: the world around you

OBJECTIVE: I can tell about the world in which I live.

TEACHER GOAL: To review what the children have learned about the world around them.

READING INTEGRATION: main idea, noting and recalling details, following written directions, writing sentences

VOCABULARY: (world, town, country)

MATERIALS NEEDED: globe, world and U.S. maps, pictures of different places in the world, pencils

TEACHING PAGES 24 and 25:

Have the children open their LIFEPACs to page 24. Discuss what they see in the picture. Ask the picture to tell what they remember about the object the girl and her dog are looking at. Name the country they are pointing to. Find it on the classroom globe and map. Have the children find and name other countries. Have them tell the name of the world we live in.

Read the page together. Discuss the question at the bottom. How many of the children can name the town and country they live in? How many know what the name of your state is?

Write the words *school, town, country, home,* and *world* on the board. Say the words together. Make sure all the children know them. Have them turn to page 25 and read the directions to themselves. Let the children do the page independently. Be available to help any children who may have difficulty with a word or a picture. Check the work together.

III. THE WORLD AROUND YOU

God made the world
in which you live.
It has many kinds of places.
Your school is in a town.
Your town is in a country.
The country is part
of the whole world.

Can you tell the name of your town and of your country?

page 24 (twenty-four)

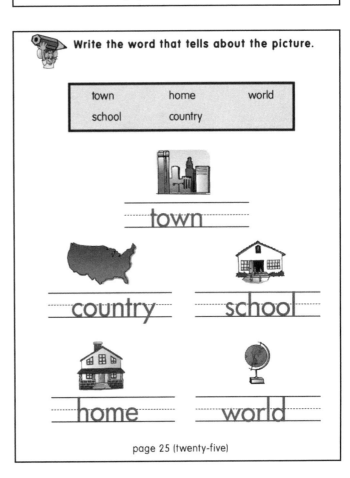

Write the word that tells about the picture.

town	home	world
school	country	

town

country   school

home   world

page 25 (twenty-five)

ACTIVITY:

Write the words *north* and *south* on the board. Ask the children to read them and tell you what each means. Review north and south as directions on a map or globe. Review all the directions in relation to the classroom. See the Teachers Handbook for Social Studies 109 page 6 for direction activities.

Pages 26 and 27: Places People Live

CONCEPT: places people live

OBJECTIVE: I can tell about the world in which I live.

TEACHER GOAL: To teach and review the various kinds of places people live.

READING INTEGRATION: main idea, noting and recalling details, following written directions, classifying

VOCABULARY: (farms, cities, sea)

MATERIALS NEEDED: Worksheet 3, crayons, pencils

TEACHING PAGES 26 and 27:

Have the children open their LIFEPACs to page 26. Read the title and ask the children to name some different places people live. Talk about the three shown on this page. Read the captions one-at-a-time and discuss what it would be like to live in that place. Have the children decide what kind of place they live in. How would they describe the place they live to someone who had never been there.

Pass out the Worksheet. Here is another kind of place people live today. Find Arizona on the map. Talk about the kind of weather this Indian family has where they live. Explain that although people usually think of Arizona as being very hot all the time, only parts of the state are like that. Where the Navajo Indians live the summers are very warm and dry but the winters are usually cold and sometimes snowy. The houses have to be built so they stay cool in the summer and can be heated easily in the winter. Many Navajos today live in more modern homes, but many still live in the old style houses known as *hogans*. Have the children describe the picture and what they see in it. If any have ever visited

PLACES PEOPLE LIVE

People live in many different places.

Some people live on farms.

Some people live in cities.

Other people live by the sea.

page 26 (twenty-six)

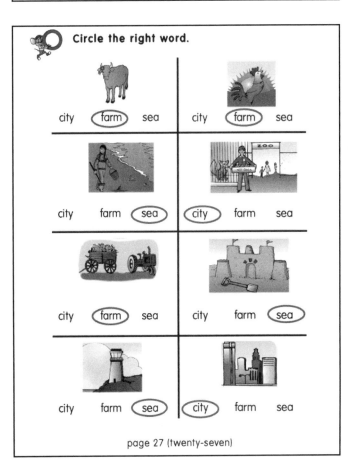

Circle the right word.

city	farm	sea	city	farm	sea
city	farm	sea	city	farm	sea
city	farm	sea	city	farm	sea
city	farm	sea	city	farm	sea

page 27 (twenty-seven)

Navajoland, now is a good time for them to share their experiences.

Have the children turn to page 27. Read the directions together. Identify any pictures that may not be clearly understood. When the children are finished check the page together and talk about the children's answers.

Name _____

To talk about and color.

This family lives in the high deserts of Arizona.

History & Geography 110
Worksheet 3
with page 27

Teacher check _____
Initial   Date

Pages 28 and 29: Your Country

CONCEPT: your country

OBJECTIVE: I can tell about the world in which I live.

TEACHER GOAL: To teach and review facts about the United States and its history.

READING INTEGRATION: main idea, noting and recalling details, following written directions, listening

VOCABULARY: (United States), beautiful, mountains, deserts, Pilgrims, America, Columbus, discovered, George Washington, President, Abraham Lincoln, Americans

MATERIALS NEEDED: crayons, pictures of historical America, pencils

TEACHING PAGES 28 and 29:

Have the children open their LIFEPACs to page 28. Discuss the picture. What is the family doing? Have the children share experiences about their family's vacation trips. Talk about some of the places they have visited. Show pictures of historical places in America. Mention any that are close to where your school is located.

Have the children read the page together and talk about it in relation to places they have been. After reading the page, tell the children to take out their crayons. Give them the following directions. Stress to them the importance of listening carefully.

1.   Find the word that means a very high place and put a *red line* under it.

2.   Put a *blue line* under the name of the people who came to America to be free to worship God in their own ways.

3.   Put a *green box* around the name of our first President.

4.   *Circle* the word that tells what the leader of America is called.

YOUR COUNTRY

God has made the United States
a very beautiful country.
It has mountains, deserts,
rivers, and lakes.
God has made our country free.
You are free to worship God.
The Pilgrims came to the
United States to worship God.

Columbus discovered America.
George Washington was the first
President.
Abraham Lincoln was another
President.
People in the United States thank
God for a free and beautiful country.

page 28 (twenty-eight)

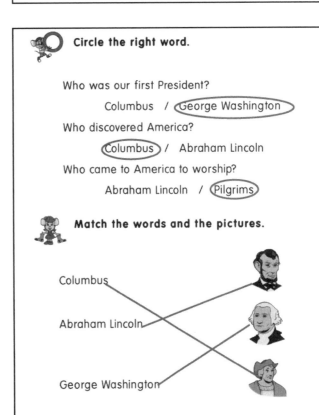

Circle the right word.

Who was our first President?

Columbus / (George Washington)

Who discovered America?

(Columbus) / Abraham Lincoln

Who came to America to worship?

Abraham Lincoln / (Pilgrims)

Match the words and the pictures.

Columbus

Abraham Lincoln

George Washington

page 29 (twenty-nine)

5. Put a *yellow line* under the name of the person who discovered America.

Have the children turn to page 29 and read the directions. When they are finished, check the page together. Review any points that caused a problem.

Pages 30 and 31: Your World

CONCEPT: your world

OBJECTIVE: I can tell about the world in which I live.

TEACHER GOAL: To teach and review facts about the world in general and Mexico and Japan in particular.

READING INTEGRATION: main idea, noting and recalling details, following written directions, speaking in a group, listening

VOCABULARY: (earth, Mexico, Japan, ocean)

MATERIAL NEEDED: writing tablet, globe, map, pencils, crayons

TEACHING PAGES 30 and 31:

Have the children open their LIFEPACs to page 30. Have the children tell about the two pictures they see at the top. Write Ikuko and Carlos on the board. Ask which country each of the two children is from. Ask which family at the top belongs to Ikuko and which one belongs to Carlos. *Ask the children:* "What are the children doing in the picture of Mexico?"

"Why do Japanese people eat sitting on the floor?"

Read the pages together and talk about them. Find the countries of Japan and Mexico on the globe and on the map. Talk about how children in Japan and Mexico are like children in America. Talk about how these children are different from American children.

Have the children finish the activity on page 31 before discussing the question at the bottom of the page. Talk about some of the fiestas that are celebrated in Mexico and some of the important holidays celebrated in Japan.

YOUR WORLD

The world you live in
is called Earth.
Earth has many different places.
People live all around the world.
Mexico is a neighbor
of the United States.
Japan is far away
across the ocean.

page 30 (thirty)

Children in Mexico and Japan
may look different,
but they are very much like you.
They play and go to school.
They have families and friends.
Best of all, many of them are your
brothers and sisters
in God's family.

Finish the dot-to-dot.

What country has fiestas?

page 31 (thirty-one)

ACTIVITY:
Have the children write a story about what it would be like to live in either Mexico or Japan. Have them illustrate their stories and share them with the class when time allows.

Page 32: Activity Page

MATERIALS NEEDED: pencils

TEACHING PAGE 32:

Have the children turn to page 32. Read the directions together for the first activity. As the children work, be available for any child who may need help with a word. Explain that in the second activity they are not looking for pictures that are just alike but kinds of things that BELONG TOGETHER, that are in some way similar. As soon as all the children are finished, check the page and discuss each answer as it is read.

Using the flashcards and word chart, review all the vocabulary words for the entire LIFEPAC. This review and practice should cover word recognition, reading the word, and being able to use the word in a sentence or tell what it means.

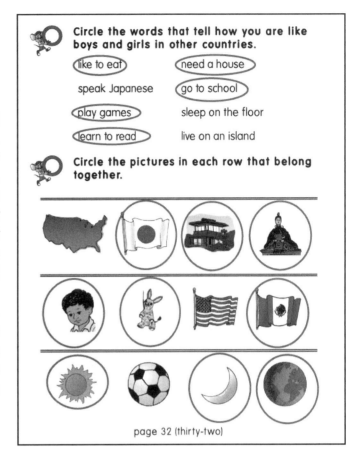

Page 33: Self Test 3

CONCEPT: evaluation

OBJECTIVE: I can tell about the world in which I live.

READING INTEGRATION: following directions, recalling details

VOCABULARY: Review all the vocabulary words.

MATERIALS NEEDED: pencils

TEACHING PAGE 33:

Have the children turn to page 33. Read the directions together. Answer any questions about what to do. Identify all the illustrations. Allow the children sufficient time to complete the page. Check the page as soon as possible after all are finished.

ACTIVITY:

Review all the concepts and facts presented in this LIFEPAC before the children take the LIFEPAC Test.

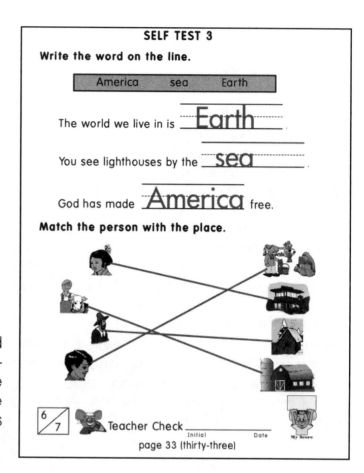

LIFEPAC TEST AND ALTERNATE LIFEPAC TEST

Administer the test to the class as a group. Ask to have directions read or read them to the class. In either case, be sure that the children clearly understand. Put examples on the board if it seems necessary. Give ample time for each activity to be completed before going to the next.

Correct immediately and discuss with the child.

Review any concepts that have been missed.

Give those children who do not achieve the 80% score additional copies of the worksheets and a list of vocabulary words to study. A parent of a classroom helper should help in the review.

When the child is ready, give the Alternate LIFEPAC Test. Use the same procedure as for the LIFEPAC TEST.

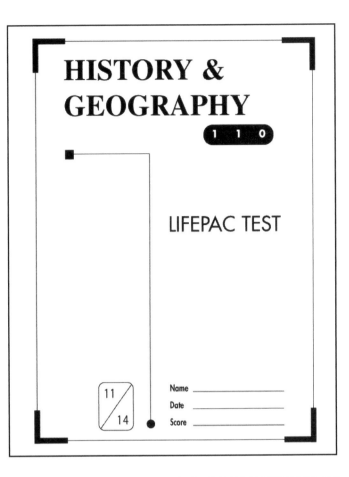

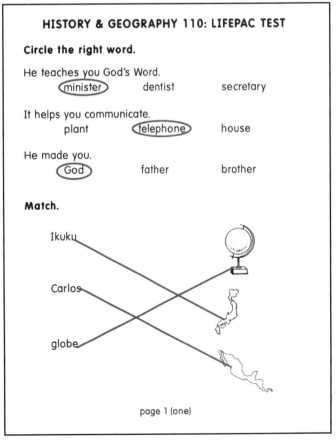

Write <u>yes</u> or <u>no</u> on the line.

People communicate. _____ yes _____

All people love God. _____ no _____

Everyone is the same. _____ no _____

God gave us laws
because He loves us. _____ yes _____

Write the word.

| missionary | symbol | sad | worship |

symbol  | worship

missionary  | sad

page 2 (two)

NOTES

page 3 (three)

HISTORY & GEOGRAPHY
1 1 0

ALTERNATE LIFEPAC TEST

12 / 15

Name _____
Date _____
Score _____

**HISTORY & GEOGRAPHY 110:
ALTERNATE LIFEPAC TEST**

Match.

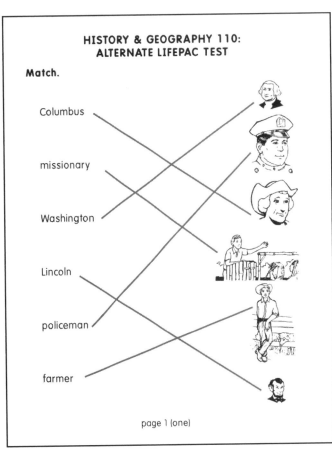

Columbus

missionary

Washington

Lincoln

policeman

farmer

page 1 (one)

Circle the word.

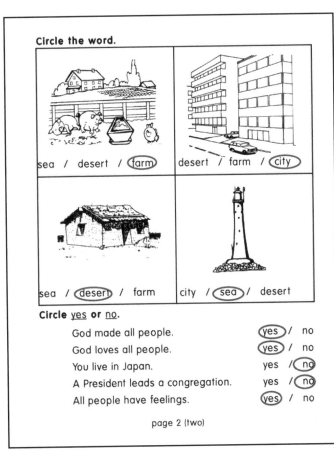

sea / desert / (farm)   desert / farm / (city)

sea / (desert) / farm   city / (sea) / desert

Circle yes or no.

God made all people.   (yes) / no
God loves all people.   (yes) / no
You live in Japan.   yes / (no)
A President leads a congregation.   yes / (no)
All people have feelings.   (yes) / no

page 2 (two)

NOTES

page 3 (three)

209

HISTORY & GEOGRAPHY 101-110: Cumulative Word List

Abraham Lincoln
across
act
address
afraid
alarm
alone
along
already
always
America
Americans
angry
animals
another
apartment
arresting
baby
baptizes
barn
baseball
basketball
beans
bear
because
begin
bells
belongs
best
Bill
Billy
blind
boat
Bobby
both
brave
breakfast
breathe
brick
brush
bucket
build
buildings
buys
calf
campfire
canicas
card
carefully
cares
Carlos

cavities
celebrated
chapel
chart
check
church
circle
cities
city
city worker
clams
claps
class
classmates
clean
clock
closer
cloth
clothes
Columbus
commandments
communicate
communicated
community
compact
congregation
cooks
copy
count
cries
crossing
crows
cry
curtains
customs
danger
day
deaf
decorations
deliver
dentist
desks
devil
different
direct
discovered
dishes
disobeyed
doctor
doing
don't

doors
dream
dressed
each
early
earns
ears
earth
Easter
energy
English
enjoys
errand
everyone
everything
evil
exactly
exercise
excuse
expects
eyes
fair
families
family
farm
favorite
fear
feast
feeds
feelings
festivals
fiesta
fifty
fight
findeth
Fireman Dan
first
fisherman
five
flash
flat
floor
flown
foghorn
follow
food
four
Francis Scott Key
free
freedom
friend

front
funny
furniture
garden
gathers
George Washington
getas
glad
globe
grade
grandma
grandparents
grow
guides
gym
happen
happy
hard
having
hayride
healthy
heart
heaven
hello
helps
helpful
helping
hole
holidays
home
hopscotch
horns
house
hug
hungry
hunt
hurt
Ikuko
important
Independence
Indians
island
it's
jacket
Japan
Japanese
Jimmy
kimono
kind
kitchen
kiss

knocked
knows
large
law
lawn
leads
leader
learning
lessons
letters
librarian
library
light
lighthouse
Lisa
list
loud
loves
lunch
made
manners
maps
marbles
marshmallows
math
Mayflower
medicine
meet
members
Mexico
Mike
mind
mine
minute
mirror
Mr. James
Mr. Riley
Mrs. Howard
Mrs. Wills
money
month
morning
mountains
mows
music
mysterious
name
needs
Nina
number
nurse
obey
ocean

office
oldest
opens
paper
paramedics
parents
park
Pastor Johnson
people
person
pictures
pigeons
Pilgrims
pillows
pinata
Pinta
play
please
Pledge of Allegiance
Plymouth
point
policeman
polite
porch
prayer
President
principal
prize
promised
protect
question
quiet
rainy
rake
ready
receive
recess
remind
report
respect
return
rhymes
right
roast
rollerskate
roof
room
rooster
route
sad
safe
sailors
sand castle

Santa Maria
school
sea
second
secretary
sentences
share
sharing
shells
shines
shingles
ships
shore
pick
signs
silent
sirens
sister
smallest
smiles
soccer
something
song
sorry
sounds
soup
Spanish
special
sport
Squanto
stand
"Star-Spangled Banner"
steps
stoplight
story
stories
straight
strangers
street
stripes
strong
summer
Sunday
sunshine
surprise
symbols
table
talk
tamales
teaches
teeth
tell

thankful
Thanksgiving
thank you
there's
third
thirteen
throat
through
time
today
together
tonight
torn
touch
tractor
traffic
trash
travel
treat
truck
tucks
twins
United States
vacuum
vegetables
very
visited
wagon
wait
wake
war
warning
wear
weather vane
week
what
where
window
winter
wisdom
wise
wonder
wood
world
worship
wrong
youngest
yourself

WORKSHEETS

Reproducible Worksheets
for use with the
History & Geography 100
Teacher's Guide

Who is in the barn?

Cut the barn door on the dotted line.

Cut out the circle.

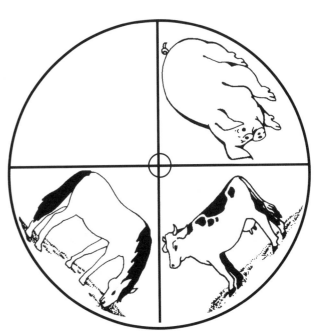

Teacher check _____

Name _____

Farm Homes

Color. Cut out. Match.

 Teacher check _____

Initial   Date

Make a rooster.
Use these shapes.
Cut them out.
Paste them on drawing paper.

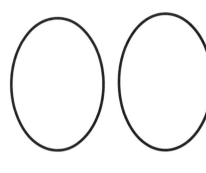

Teacher check _____

Initial   Date

What is in the garden?
Connect the dots.

② ① ⑮ ⑭

④ ⑫ ⑬

⑤ ⑪

⑧

⑥ ⑩

⑦ ⑨

Unscramble this word.

CSARECRWO

_____

- -

_____

History & Geography 106
Worksheet 4
with page 4

Teacher check _____

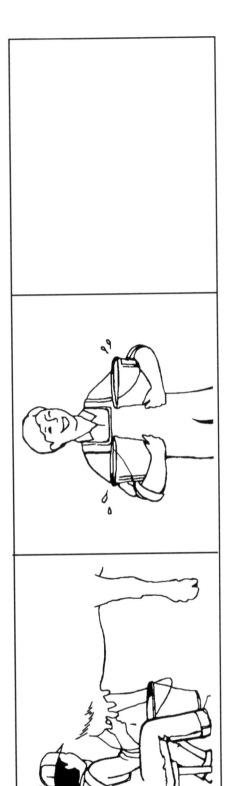

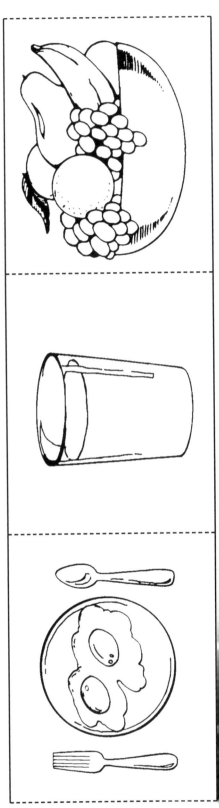

History & Geography 106
Worksheet 5
with page 5

 Teacher check _____

Initial   Date

Name _____

One or More?

_____

- - - - - - - - - - - - - - - - -

_____

_____

- - - - - - - - - - - - - - - - -

_____

_____

- - - - - - - - - - - - - - - - -

_____

Words to use:

cow	chicks	hens	boy	chick	egg
hen	boys	eggs	pig	pigs	cows

History & Geography 106
Worksheet 6
with page 5

Teacher check _____

Initial   Date

Name _____

Color. Cut out.

fold on dotted line

Teacher check _____

Initial   Date

Name _____

Puzzle Paste.

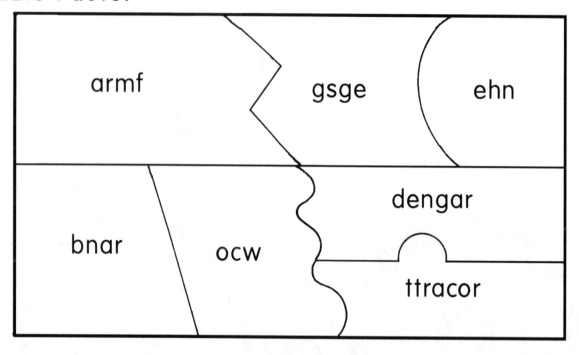

armf   gsge   ehn

bnar   ocw   dengar   ttracor

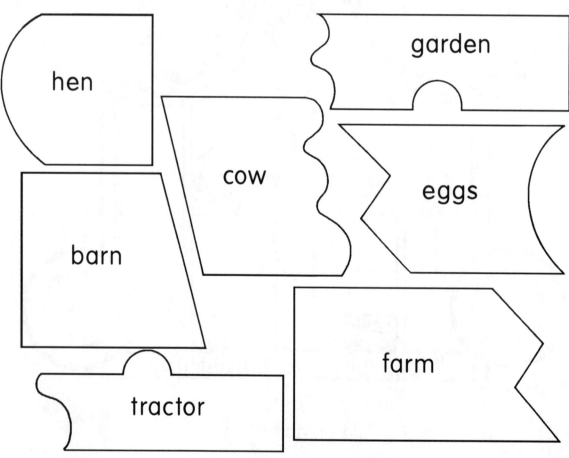

hen   garden

cow   eggs

barn

tractor   farm

Teacher check _____

Initial   Date

Name _____

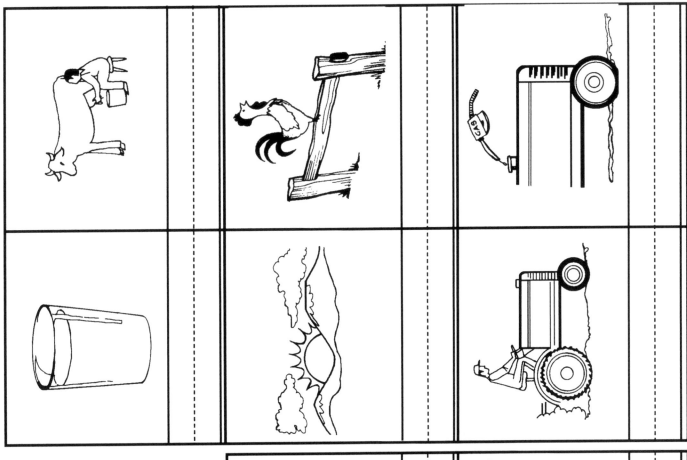

Write
before **and** after.

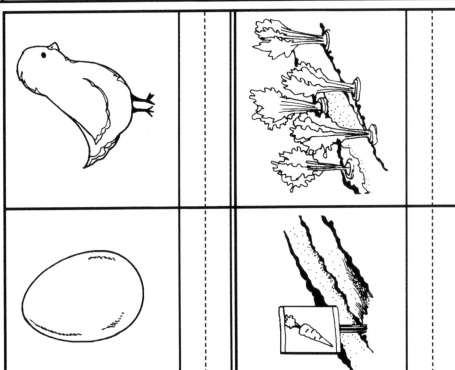

History & Geography 106
Worksheet 9
with page 6

Teacher check _____

Initial   Date

223

Finger Puppets

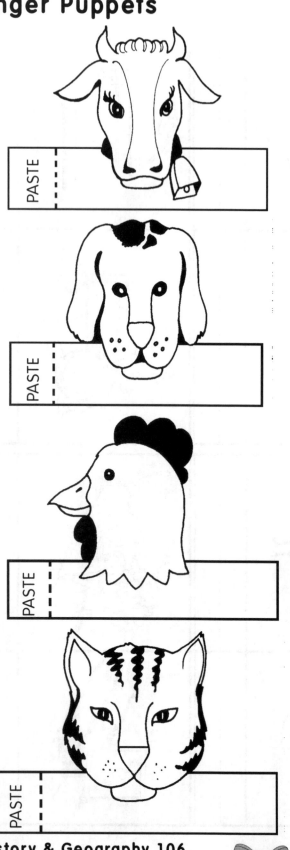

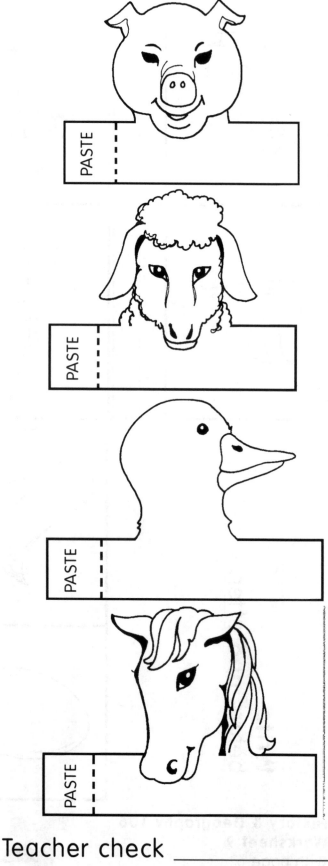

History & Geography 106
Worksheet 10
with page 11

Teacher check _____

Initial   Date

224

Name _____

House Numbers

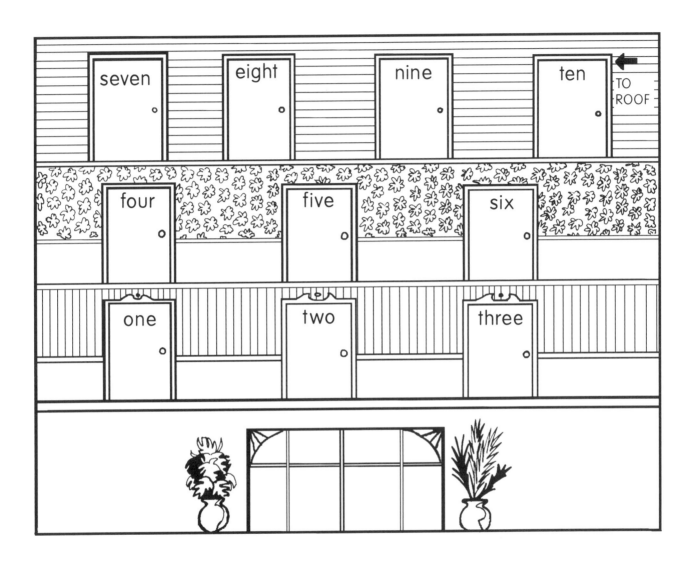

Cut. Paste the numbers on the right door.

3	9	6	1	10	7	8	5	4	2

Teacher check _____
                  Initial   Date

Name _____

 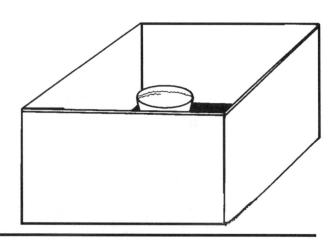

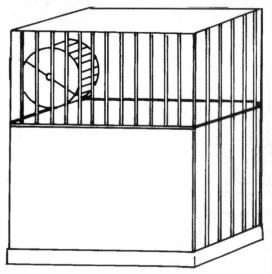 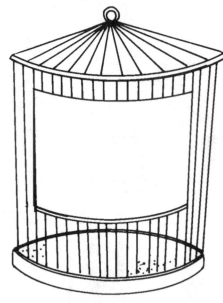

Teacher check _____

Initial   Date

Name _____

City Wheels

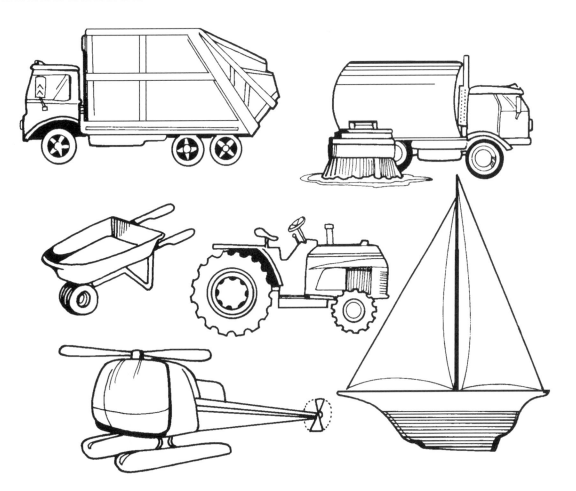

Teacher check _____

Initial   Date

227

Sweep up the words.

← cut →

trash

crash

dash

mash

wash

flash

sash

dish

fish

History & Geography 106
Worksheet 14
with page 16-17

Teacher check _____

Initial   Date

228

Play Zoo Keeper

Game card #1 | Game card #2

SET TWO

SET ONE

Teacher check _____

Initial   Date

Name _____

PLACE THE CAGES

1. Put the elephant below the bird cage.

2. Put the lion above the zebras.

3. Put the monkey beside the pond.

History & Geography 106
Worksheet 16
with page 18

Teacher check _____

Initial   Date

230

Name _____

Cut out

PULL

cut

cut

History & Geography 106
Worksheet 17
with page 23

Teacher check _____

Initial   Date

231

Name _____

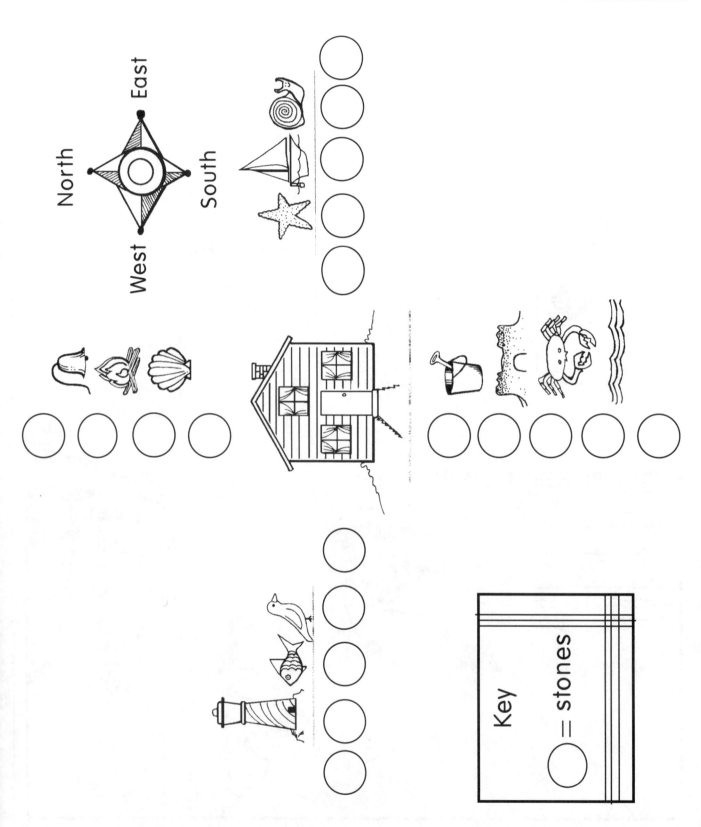

History & Geography 106
Worksheet 18
with page 27

Teacher check _____
Initial   Date

232

Name _____

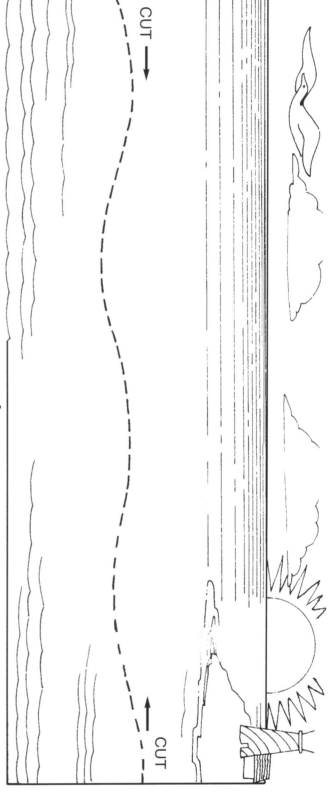

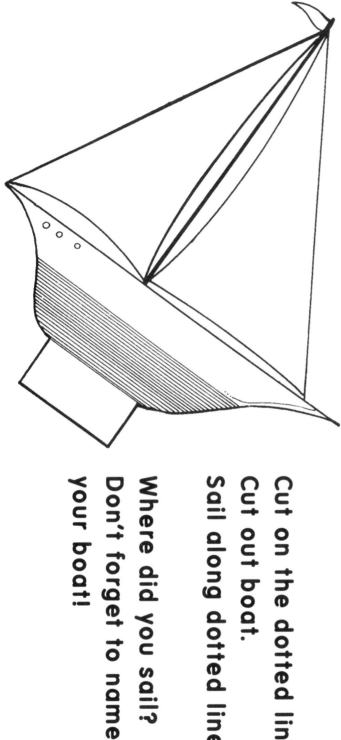

Cut on the dotted line.
Cut out boat.
Sail along dotted line.

Where did you sail?
Don't forget to name
your boat!

History & Geography 106
Worksheet 19
with page 28

Teacher check _____

Initial   Date

233

Name _____

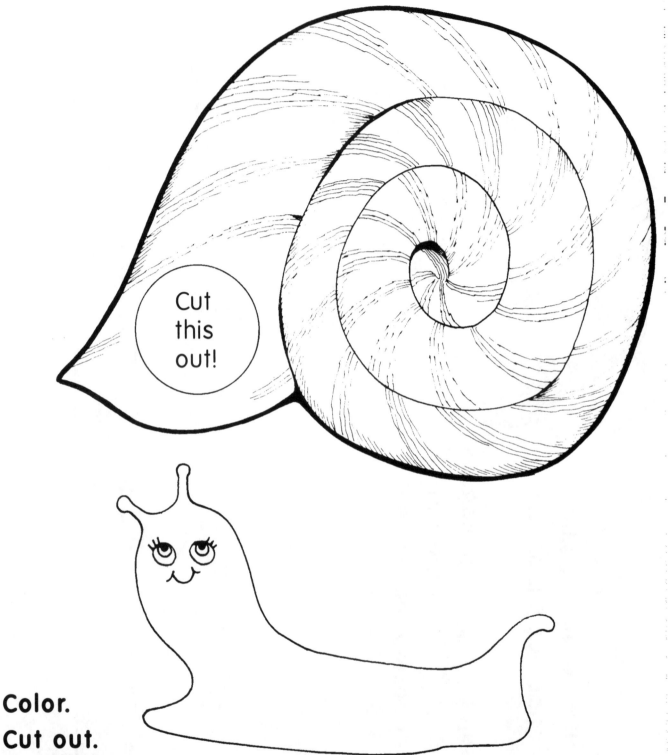

Cut
this
out!

Color.

Cut out.

Put head through circle.

History & Geography 106
Worksheet 20
with page 29

Teacher check _____

Initial   Date

234

Name _____

 Talk about other ways policemen and firemen help each other.

 Teacher check _____

Initial   Date

Fire Fighting of Long Ago

1776

1900

 In what ways is firefighting today different from long ago?

History & Geography 107
Worksheet 2
with page 5

 Teacher check _____
Initial   Date

236

Forest rangers are policemen **and** firemen.
They protect people and wildlife.

History & Geography 107
Worksheet 3
with page 9

Teacher check _____

Initial   Date

Name _____

Write <u>yes</u> by the children who are taking care of themselves.

History & Geography 107
Worksheet 4
with page 13

Teacher check _____

Initial   Date

238

Name _____

What will come next?

History & Geography 107
Worksheet 5
with page 17

Teacher check _____
                                    Initial   Date

239

Name _____

Match the word with the picture.

teeth

city worker

litterbug

dentist

medicine

nurse

Teacher check _____

Initial   Date

Name _____

Tell if the book is fact or fantasy.

ALL ABOUT TRUCKS — fact fantasy	Three Billy Goats Gruff — fact fantasy
LIFEPAC Community Helper — fact fantasy	HOLY BIBLE — fact fantasy
Winnie-the-pooh — fact fantasy	CINDERELLA — fact fantasy

History & Geography 107
Worksheet 7
with page 29

Teacher check _____

Initial   Date

241

Turkey Patterns

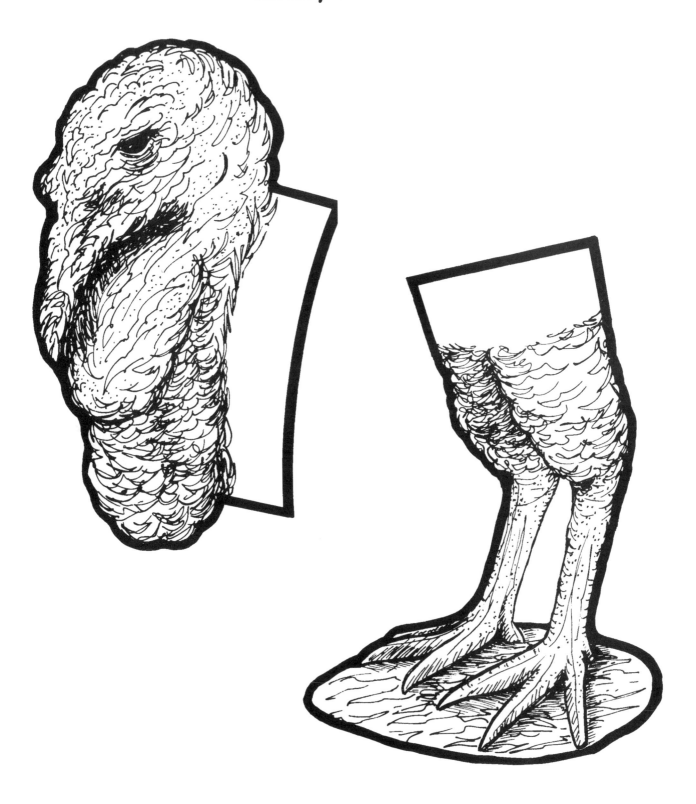

History & Geography 108
Worksheet 1
with page 9

Teacher check _____

Initial   Date

243

Match the words and the pictures.

United States

Indians

Columbus

Pilgrims

Plymouth

ship

History & Geography 108
Worksheet 2
with page 11

Teacher check _____

Initial   Date

244

Going to school in colonial days.

The children read their lessons from boards called **hornbooks.**

Teacher check _____

Initial   Date

Abe Lincoln loved to read and learn.
He borrowed books from anyone who would loan him one.

Abe Lincoln was honest and a hard worker.
Once a book he borrowed was ruined in the rain.
He worked 3 days to pay for the book.

History & Geography 108
Worksheet 4
with page 19

Teacher check _____

Initial   Date

Name _____

Find the right word and write it on the line.

flag	Pilgrim	president
Indian	pledge	United States

_____

_____

_____

_____

_____

_____

History & Geography 108
Worksheet 5
with page 29

Teacher check _____
Initial   Date

247

Johnny Appleseed
Draw what happens next.

Johnny plants apple seeds.

Johnny waters tiny trees.

History & Geography 108
Worksheet 6
with page 31

Teacher check _____

Initial   Date

248

Finding Directions

Teacher check _____

Initial   Date

Name _____

Write the word on the line.

WORD	mountains	globe
BOX	country	north

_____

- - - - - - - - - - - - - - - - - - -

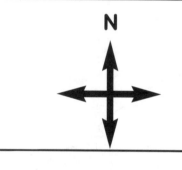

_____

- - - - - - - - - - - - - - - - - - -

Write the words in alphabetical order.

rainy   _____

               - - - - - - - - - - - - - - - - - - -

world   _____

               - - - - - - - - - - - - - - - - - - -

south   _____

               - - - - - - - - - - - - - - - - - - -

History & Geography 109
Worksheet 2
with page 9

Teacher check _____

Initial   Date

250

Name _____

Discuss the picture and color it.

This Mexican family is on their way to the market place.

Teacher check _____

Initial   Date

World Friends Mobile

FRIENDS AROUND
THE
WORLD

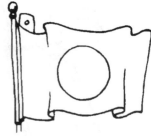

Directions

Color pictures.

Cut out pictures.

Tie pictures with

string as in the picture.

History & Geography 109
Worksheet 4
with page 27

Teacher check _____

Initial   Date

Name _____

ORIGAMI PATTERN

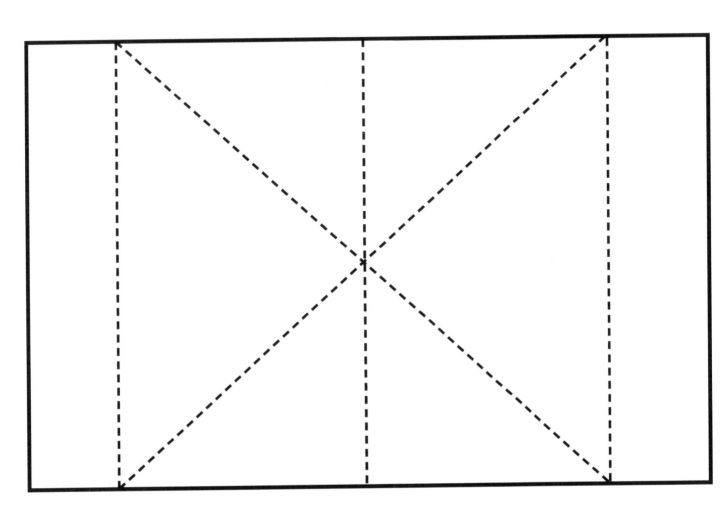

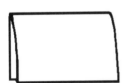

1. cut on solid
lines
fold on center
dotted line

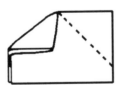

2. fold forward
on dotted
lines

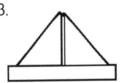

3. fold upon
bottom dotted
lines

4. clip corners
and draw or
paint snow
at the top

History & Geography 109
Worksheet 5
with page 27

Teacher check _____

Initial   Date

Name _____

Write a sentence telling where Ikuko lives.

_____
- -
_____

_____
- -
_____

How many days a week do you go to school?

_____
- -
_____

_____
- -
_____

Write a sentence tell about the house in which you live.

_____
- -
_____

_____
- -
_____

History & Geography 109
Worksheet 6
with page 29

Teacher check _____
                Initial   Date

254

Name _____

Color and discuss the picture.

Boys' Day in Japan

History & Geography 109
Worksheet 7
with page 31

Teacher check _____

Initial   Date

255

Name _____

Write the number of the word next to the right sentence.

1. communicate   4. sound
2. special   5. silent
3. feelings   6. family

_____ You are part of these.

_____ This is the way each person is to God.

_____ When you cry, you show these.

_____ You do this when you call someone on the telephone.

_____ This is the way the world seems to a deaf person.

_____ When you sing, you make this.

History & Geography 110
Worksheet 1
with page 9

Teacher check _____

Initial   Date

Finish the face.
Make a puppet.

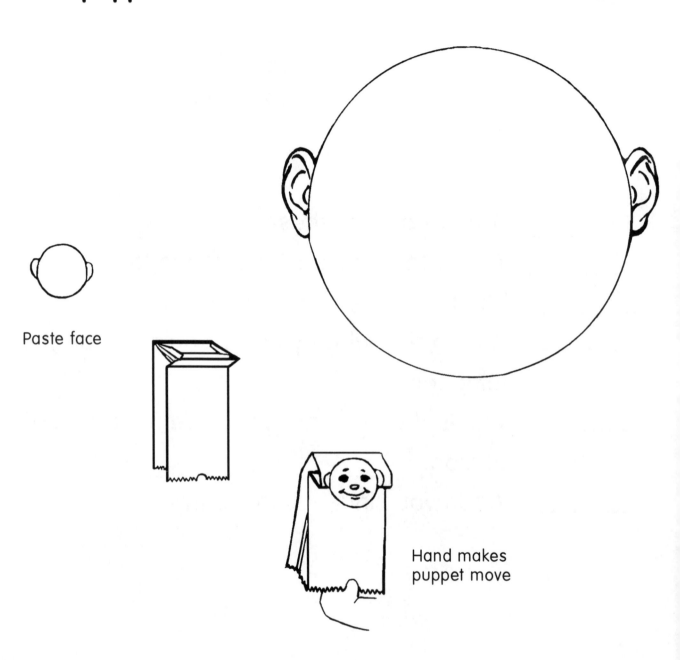

Paste face

Hand makes
puppet move

History & Geography 110
Worksheet 2
with page 12

Teacher check _____
Initial   Date

258

To talk about and color.

This family lives in the high deserts of Arizona.

History & Geography 110
Worksheet 3
with page 27

Teacher check _____
Initial   Date

259

T E S T S

Reproducible Tests
for use with the
History & Geography 100
Teacher's Guide

HISTORY & GEOGRAPHY

106

ALTERNATE
LIFEPAC TEST

Name _____

Date _____

Score _____

HISTORY & GEOGRAPHY 106: ALTERNATE LIFEPAC TEST

EACH ANSWER, 1 POINT

Match.

Farm

City

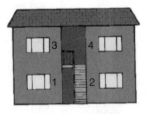

Sea

page 1 (one)

Circle the picture that best completes each sentence.

Lisa will _____ .

Ships see light from the _____ .

Use these words to complete the sentences.

shells   **ball**   **chores**   **zoo**

Children in the city like to go to the _____.

Stanley likes to play _____ with his family.

Josh collects _____.

Stanley, Lisa, and Josh all have to do_____.

NOTES

HISTORY & GEOGRAPHY

1 0 7

ALTERNATE LIFEPAC TEST

8 / 11

Name _____

Date _____

Score _____

HISTORY & GEOGRAPHY 107:
ALTERNATE LIFEPAC TEST

Match the sentences and pictures.

Who teaches about
God's love?

Who lends books?

Who fills cavities?

Who gives medicine?

Who cleans streets?

Who puts out fires?

Who protects wildlife.

Circle the child who is helping each worker.

NOTES

HISTORY & GEOGRAPHY

1 0 8

ALTERNATE
LIFEPAC TEST

10 / 13

Name _____

Date _____

Score _____

HISTORY & GEOGRAPHY 108: ALTERNATE LIFEPAC TEST

Write 1, 2, 3 to show what happened first, second, and third.

_____

_____

_____

Write the right word.

Squanto was the_____ friend.

President's / Pilgrim's

Columbus had _____ ships.

one / two / three

The Mayflower Compact was a list of _____.

people / rules

Circle <u>yes</u> **or** <u>no</u>.

Rules and laws protect people.   yes   /   no

The first President was Lincoln.   yes   /   no

You can say the Pledge of
Allegiance   yes   /   no

Match the names and the pictures.

Squanto

Lincoln

Washington

United States

NOTES

HISTORY & GEOGRAPHY

1 0 9

ALTERNATE LIFEPAC TEST

Name _____

Date _____

Score _____

HISTORY & GEOGRAPHY 109:
ALTERNATE LIFEPAC TEST

Circle the right word.

 | 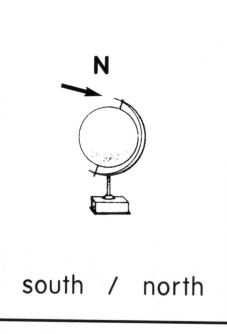 |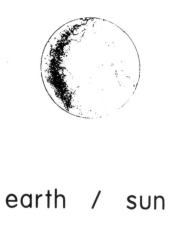

globe / pole | south / north | earth / sun

**Circle the groups of words that tell ways
Ikuko, Carlos, and you are different.**

language   go to school

play fames   play with friends

food you eat   clothes you wear

Circle <u>yes</u> **or** <u>no</u>**.**

God made all people the same on the inside.
yes / no

page 1 (one)

Circle the right word.

Mexico is a _____ country.
　　　　　　　　　cold　/　hot

Japan has many tall _____.
　　　　　　　　　mountains　/　buildings

The _____ is round.
　　　globe　/　map

Japan is _____ than Mexico.
　　　　　bigger　/　smaller

Match the house with the country.

United States

Japan

Mexico

NOTES

HISTORY & GEOGRAPHY

110

ALTERNATE LIFEPAC TEST

| 12 / 15 |

Name _____

Date _____

Score _____

HISTORY & GEOGRAPHY 110:
ALTERNATE LIFEPAC TEST

Match.

Columbus

missionary

Washington

Lincoln

policeman

farmer

page 1 (one)

Circle the word.

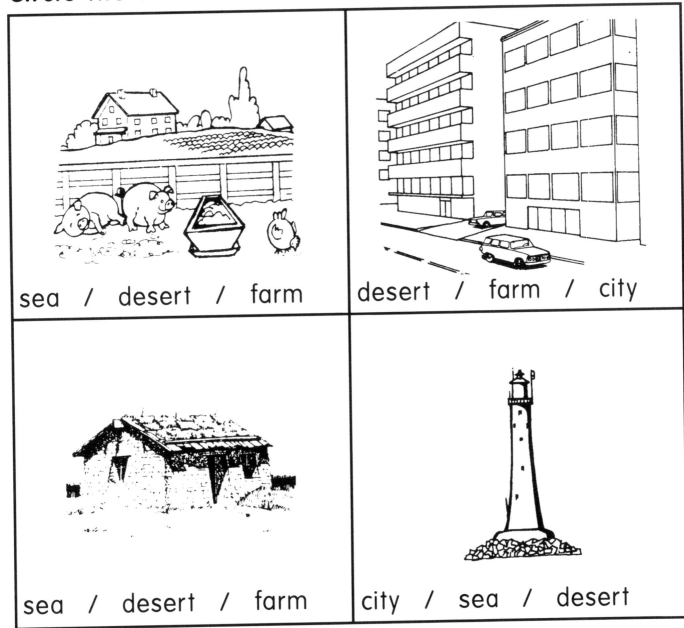

sea / desert / farm

desert / farm / city

sea / desert / farm

city / sea / desert

Circle <u>yes</u> **or** <u>no</u>.

God made all people.	yes / no
God loves all people.	yes / no
You live in Japan.	yes / no
A President leads a congregation.	yes / no
All people have feelings.	yes / no

page 2 (two)

NOTES